T0269941

JOHN BERGER

My Reading

IONA HEATH

JOHN BERGER

Ways of Learning

OXFORD
UNIVERSITY PRESS

OXFORD
UNIVERSITY PRESS

Great Clarendon Street, Oxford, OX2 6DP,
United Kingdom

Oxford University Press is a department of the University of Oxford.
It furthers the University's objective of excellence in research, scholarship,
and education by publishing worldwide. Oxford is a registered trade mark of
Oxford University Press in the UK and in certain other countries

Published in the United States of America by Oxford University Press
198 Madison Avenue, New York, NY 10016, United States of America

British Library Cataloguing in Publication Data
Data available

Library of Congress Control Number: 2023951548

ISBN 9780192864239

DOI: 10.1093/oso/9780192864239.001.0001

Printed and bound in the UK by
Clays Ltd, Elcograf S.p.A.

SERIES INTRODUCTION

This series is built on a simple presupposition: that it helps to have a book recommended and discussed by someone who cares for it. Books are not purely self-sufficient: they need people and they need to get to what is personal within them.

The people we have been seeking as contributors to *My Reading* are readers who are also writers: novelists and poets; literary critics, outside as well as inside universities, but also thinkers from other disciplines—philosophy, psychology, science, theology, and sociology—beside the literary; and, not least of all, intense readers whose first profession is not writing itself but, for example, medicine, or law, or a non-verbal form of art. Of all of them we have asked: what books or authors feel as though they are deeply *yours*, influencing or challenging your life and work, most deserving of rescue and attention, or demanding of feeling and use?

What is it like to love this book? What is it like to have a thought or idea or doubt or memory, not cold and in abstract, but live in the very act of reading? What is it like to feel, long after, that this writer is a vital part of your life? We ask our authors to respond to such bold questions by writing not conventionally but personally—whatever 'personal' might mean, whatever form or style it might take, for them as individuals. This does not mean overt confession at the expense of a chosen book or author; but nor should our writers be afraid of making autobiographical connections. What was wanted was whatever made for their own hardest thinking in careful relation to quoted sources and specifics. The work was to go on in the taut and resonant space between these readers and their chosen books. And the interest within that area begins precisely when it is no longer clear how much is coming from the text and how much is coming from its readers—where that distinction is no longer easily tenable because neither is sacrificed to the other. That would show what reading meant at its most serious and how it might have relation to an individual life.

Out of what we hope will be an ongoing variety of books and readers, *My Reading* offers personal models of what it is like to care about particular authors, to recreate through specific examples imaginative versions of what those authors and works represent, and to show their effect upon a reader's own thinking and development.

ANNE CHENG

PHILIP DAVIS

JACQUELINE NORTON

MARINA WARNER

MICHAEL WOOD

For Maria Nadotti, who John called Angel

CONTENTS

CONTENTS

LIST OF ILLUSTRATIONS

'There comes a time when you have to stop reading and start writing'

John Berger
Antony
July 2016

PART ONE
BEGINNINGS

1

MEETING

I met John Berger on 27 January 2000. He had been persuaded to give a talk at the Royal College of General Practitioners and he had taken some convincing. At the time I was a member of the committee which nominated people for awards and eponymous lectures. For this particular lecture, I remember people suggesting Tony Blair or Prince Philip and my heart sank. I asked whether this lecture was only to do with public prestige or whether we wanted to think more deeply about general practice and its role in society.

I had been introduced to John's writing through *A Fortunate Man* which I had read as an undergraduate medical student back in 1969. When I read it for a second time twenty years later, I had no idea how my younger self could have understood any of it because, on this second occasion, I found my fifteen years of practising as a doctor resonating with the text on almost every page. Yet I must have misjudged my younger self and I am convinced that reading this book in some way determined my choice of general practice, which I have never regretted for a moment.

I attended the crucial 1998 committee meeting having just read John's book *Photocopies*, published in 1996, where I had been disturbed to read:

I have come to mistrust most doctors because they no longer really love people.[1]

I argued that the College had a responsibility to try to understand how the author of *A Fortunate Man* could have come to this state of mistrust. I won the day and a formal letter was dispatched inviting John to give the lecture.

There was no reply.

In desperation I wrote personally[2] urging him to accept the invitation and referring to what he had written in *Photocopies*:

> For someone who understood so clearly the role and power of trust in the relationship between patient and doctor, this is a damning and disturbing indictment. You write of loss of love and seem to be recognising a sense of disengagement in us which we have perhaps not yet properly recognised or come to terms with in ourselves but which has perhaps been a powerful part of the morale crisis which followed the Thatcherite 'reforms' of the health service. Have we disengaged, if so why and what could we and should we be doing about it?

Again, there seemed to be no response but a few weeks later the telephone rang one Sunday lunchtime and it was John. He told me that he couldn't give a lecture, he could only tell stories. I said that would be perfect and, to my great joy and relief, he agreed to come and even to bring with him his friend and collaborator, the brilliant photographer Jean Mohr.

---

[1] Berger, J. *Photocopies*. Bloomsbury Publishing, 1996, p. 104
[2] 15 November 1998.

A short while later, I received a letter in a handwriting that was to become very familiar. He wrote:[3]

> Of course I'll come if you think I can offer something. I'm a bit intimidated by the idea of a Lecture about general practice or the ethical questions surrounding it. ... I'm a kind of nomad—and nomads can sometimes tell stories but they're not very strong about lecturing. Yes let's try to find some way—I think I owe it to John Sassall.[4]

The actual event took place little over a year later and Marshall Marinker, the foundation chair in general practice at the University of Leicester and a thoughtful and provocative writer and thinker about general practice, provided this report for the *British Journal of General Practice*:

> The President introduced John Berger as our John Hunt Lecturer with Sir Denis's trademark sense of occasion—a cocktail of sanctity and imminent crisis. It was not an inappropriate introduction. The man who bounded onto the platform seemed at once to reassure and threaten: a Picasso perhaps, or a Hemingway or a Casals. Big, built like a bull, romantic, bohemian even in his open-necked shirt, he grabbed the mike and roamed around like a beast sniffing the air for his prey.
>
> 'If you are going to wear a white shirt don't put on a red vest underneath.' The audience tittered nervously. 'This is what you say to a child of six?' He paused, seeking agreement. 'And to a seventy-five-year-old man.' A powerful fist shot out to a woman in the front row, and then stabbed at his own barrel chest: 'That is what she just said to me.' And there, in the brilliant economy of this less than classical opening to a College

---

[3] 23 November 1998.

[4] John Sassall was the pseudonym that John Berger gave to the Fortunate Man.

grand event, the whole thesis of the evening was laid out before us: continuities, intimacy, surprise—the essence of general practice.

He thought the term 'general practice' important and good. The word 'practice' was warm and open: 'theory' was a cold and closed word. There was no script, only a table set out with open books and papers, which he picked up, examined as though he was somewhat puzzled to find them there at all, and he read from them. He read poetry by poets I had not heard of before, but ached to read now. He told tales as terrifyingly true as any ghost story.

We were offered no title, no tidy shape, no neat thesis and antithesis, no linear argument. There was, though, something disturbingly familiar about what was going on. Recognising the style was a shock: Berger was an anatomy demonstrator, holding up for our instruction specimens preserved from a long discipline of looking, listening, and imagining. What had been dissected for us here, however, was not a dead body, but a life.

Afterwards at the drinks reception there were sheepish grins of incomprehension on some faces and looks of wonderment and gratitude on others. I thought it a rapturous celebration of our deepest virtues. These are uncomfortable times. But, in having John Berger as our Millennial John Hunt Lecturer, we can count ourselves a Fortunate College.[5]

As one of those who were filled with wonderment and gratitude, this captured the event perfectly, perhaps particularly the reference to the 'long discipline of looking, listening, and imagining'.

I had tentatively brought along my, by now treasured, undergraduate copy of A Fortunate Man and I plucked up the courage to ask him to sign it and this is what he did:

[5] 'The Back Pages'. *British Journal of General Practice*. 2000, 50(452): 249–264.

Figure 1 Photograph by Jean Mohr annotated by John Berger
Source: © John Berger and John Berger Estate and Jean Mohr and Heirs of Jean Mohr.

I was thrilled and later understood how entirely characteristic of John the crucial question mark was: the generous appreciation of the other person, yet always questioning and opening the way to new ideas.

The following evening, after having cycled to and from my work at the practice in Kentish Town two and a half miles away, I wrote to John:[6]

> Yesterday was a very good day and it is already beginning to feel a bit like a dream. The great advantage of cycling, apart from reducing my poisoning of the planet, is that it gives me the time and opportunity to think—and I have wonderful and brilliant thoughts—but, sadly, like dreams, they have almost always disappeared by the time I find myself with the opportunity to write.
>
> What I have left from today's cycling is that general practitioners have always valued what we call 'continuity of care' and that we have tended to think of this in terms of accompanying the patient on a journey or witnessing a life story—both of which seem to have some validity—but what you seemed to be saying was different—you seemed to suggest that continuity is itself a dimension of health and that doctors can be part of and emphasise the continuity that runs through a life even through the dislocation of illness. But that brings me back to the things you were saying about photographs in 'Another Way of Telling'—there you seemed almost to be saying that a photograph is a dislocation of continuity—as an illness is a dislocation of the continuity of a life. And our consultations are almost like photographs of the patient's life—they enable us to draw conclusions from a short, isolated moments taken from the continuum. So we have two sorts of discontinuity—the illness and the consultation—superimposed—from which we attempt to fashion meaning:
>
>> When we give meaning to an event, that meaning is a response, not only to the known, but also to the unknown: meaning and mystery are inseparable and neither can exist

without the passing of time. Certainty may be instantaneous, doubt requires duration: meaning is born of the two.[7]

And then to the duplicity of words and your dream[8] which seemed to be about the need to touch the word, or the object of the word, from inside, to give the word the capacity to carry truth. Seamus Heaney said something similar about translating Beowulf—he said a translator has to find his own words, words which can carry his own truth, if the translation is to work.

I'm not sure about your claim that all writers ever do is sweep up a bit around the chaos—I think what you do, at least for me, is send a beam of light into the dark heart of the chaos, which may be very narrow or very short-lived but which always lets me glimpse things in a slightly different, richer way.

As I feared, this doesn't seem as lucid as it did on the bike! But it was wonderful to meet you and to listen to you and frustrating to have so little time to talk, and I hope there will be another chance.

I was trying to express the exhilaration of actively using the words of others to stimulate and enrich one's thinking about one's own everyday work: in this case John's words and my attempted care of patients, mediated by my bicycle.

A few days later, a letter from John arrived. It included:

Just got your letter. I think what I was trying to say is that the sense of psychic and physical dislocations brought about by illness or fear of illness can be lessened or even repaired when nevertheless a sense of continuity is encouraged and developed. Photographs and 'consultations' is a very rich comparison—maybe worth pursuing, no?

Later, I learnt how distinctive that closing 'No?' was inviting dissent and nonetheless fundamentally encouraging.

---

[7] Berger, J., and Mohr, J. *Another Way of Telling*. Granta Books, 1989, p. 89.
[8] Now of course, but very sadly, I can't remember the detail of the dream that John recounted in the lecture.

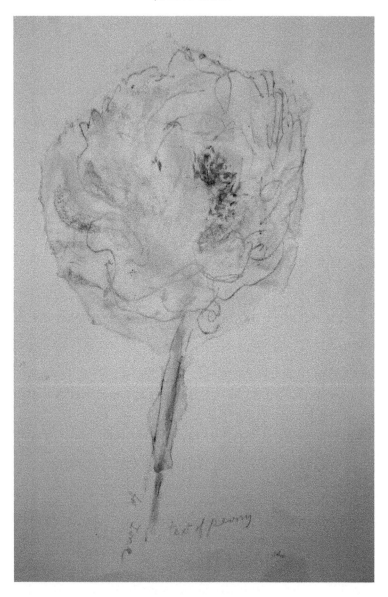

Figure 2 Drawing of a peony by John Berger
Source: © John Berger and John Berger Estate.

This was the beginning of a correspondence and a friendship which became another of the treasures of my life: a correspondence of more than 150 letters which extended over the best part of twenty years until his death in 2017. John's letters were always handwritten—some long, some short—but each contained a gift of some sort—a suggestion of a book or a poet or a musician, a question which opened my eyes, a draft of a new piece of writing, a poem or a drawing.

While I was slowly writing the small book which became *Matters of Life and Death* in English and, translated by Maria Nadotti, *Modi di Morire* in Italian, he gently pointed me in the direction of Simone Weil and Gilles Deleuze and, most importantly of all, Baruch Spinoza, none of whom had I ever read.

I remember that Deleuze describes both Foucault and Spinoza as *vivants-voyants* for whom the capacity of penetrating sight allows the 'seer' to span 'science and literature, or the imaginary and the scientific, or the known and the lived':[9]

> In the reproach that Hegel will make to Spinoza, that he ignored the negative and its power, lies the glory and innocence of Spinoza, his own discovery. In a world consumed by the negative, he has enough confidence in life, in the power of life, to challenge death, the murderous appetite of men, the rules of good and evil, of the just and the unjust. Enough confidence in life to denounce all the phantoms of the negative. … For Spinoza is one of the *vivants-voyants*. Spinoza did not believe in hope or even in courage; he believed only in joy, and in vision. He let others live, provided that others let him live. He wanted only to inspire, to waken, to reveal.[10]

I have no doubt that John should be regarded as another such *vivant-voyant*.

[9] Deleuze, G. *Foucault*. Paris: Editions Minuit, 1986.
[10] Deleuze, G. *Spinoza: Practical Philosophy*. San Francisco: City Lights Books, 1988.

He trusted my commitment to, and knowledge of, biomedical science, and never sought to trespass on that arena but he taught me almost everything else that a doctor needs to know, about the deeply human context within which medicine must be practiced, about the importance and strength of relationships, about the responsibility for respect and equity, and the recognition and acknowledgement of suffering and fear, and about the timeliness and inevitability of death.

2

BECOMING A DOCTOR

I was born eighteen months after the beginning of the National Health Service and its existence not only saved my life when I was five years old but was a big part of what made me want to be a doctor. I would not have wanted all the moral dilemmas that arise when a doctor has to take payment directly from patients for providing healthcare. I did not want to have to ask myself 'Can this patient afford the treatment that she needs?' 'What will she have to go without in order to find the money for this?' I wanted to work for the National Health Service and to help to realize that magnificent political response to the privations and suffering of the Second World War: the social generosity and solidarity of providing healthcare funded through general taxation and free at the point of need, from cradle to grave.[1]

I cannot remember a time when I did not plan to be a doctor or ever think of being anything else, which might have been something to do with my complete lack of talent in many other directions. My mother was told that it was not worth my continuing to go to dance classes when I was only four, and by six, at my first primary school, I was obliged to be the Virgin Mary in the Christmas tableau so that I didn't spoil the singing. This made such a

---

[1] Rivett, G. *From Cradle to Grave: Fifty Years of the NHS*. King's Fund, 1998.

deep impression that I can still remember the name of the boy who was cast as Joseph for the same reason. When I was fourteen, my mother was told that it was pointless to continue to pay for piano lessons, and at about the same age, I was advised to give up going to school art classes and try needlework instead.

I suppose that needing emergency surgery when I was five might have had something to do with my resolve but I don't remember ever making any such clear connection. My memories are hazy but I recall that my parents had visitors that day and we were all to go out for a country walk. I have the impression that my father was in the house which was unusual. He was in the navy and was often away for a long time. I am sure there were tensions around because by my sixth birthday my father had left for good and the bitter disputes over the divorce, custody, access, and financial support arrangements ground on over many of the following years. I have no recollection of him ever visiting me in hospital.

At the time I was only thinking about myself. I had a horrible pain and I had locked myself in the toilet. I remember people shouting and banging on the door but I don't remember opening it and nor our family doctor visiting although I'm sure he did. Yet I retain a vivid impression of the twenty-mile drive with my mother to the hospital. By this time, it was dark and we saw a fox in the headlights but I probably only remember this because my mother drew a picture of the fox for me later when I was recovering in hospital. I was diagnosed with appendicitis and my mother was told that the operation would take less than an hour. Four hours later, my mother must have been in a state approaching panic. They did not find appendicitis but took out my appendix for good measure. I had Meckel's diverticulitis and intussusception. Named after Johann Friedrich Meckel, a German anatomist born in 1809, the diverticulum is a small bulge in the small intestine that is left over from the human embryo's early connection to the yolk sac. Usually this disappears completely by the ninth week of the pregnancy but a remnant remains in approximately 2 per cent of the population and in twice as many boys as girls. Very rarely, this swelling becomes inflamed and even more rarely it triggers the small intestine to roll in on itself like a collapsible walking stick. This is a bit of a catastrophe because it very effectively cuts off the blood supply to the bowel causing gangrene. No wonder I had pain. I was later told that I had to have six of my thirty-two feet of small intestine removed so, again, no wonder the operation took longer than expected. I remember two other things: waiting desperately to see my mother during the very limited afternoon visiting hours of the 1950s and having a blood transfusion. I had a large needle in my arm with a huge bandage and a splint and I am convinced that the nurse told me that if I moved my arm, I would die. Can this possibly be true?

My mother did very well at school and was planning to apply to medical school when the Second World War broke out. Instead, she joined the Women's Royal Naval Service, met my father and married him after knowing him for only six weeks, which turned out to be less than a good idea. All her early ambitions were thwarted and exactly how much she encouraged me to fulfil them in her place I will never really know. I was never aware of any pressure but I know she took pleasure in my choice of career.

3

READING AND REREADING

When I read *A Fortunate Man* for the second time in 1989, I was in the midst of a life-changing process of rediscovering the power of literature. I had read a lot as a child and I still remember that sense of wickedness, laced with the fear of discovery, when taking advantage of the light of long summer evenings to continue reading long after I was supposed to be asleep. But as the demands of secondary school and university began to bite, I was obliged to give up reading for pleasure almost entirely. I still think that the bizarre notion that children wanting to be doctors need only study science from the age of fifteen has done terrible damage to the practice of medicine in the United Kingdom. University and medical school were quickly followed by the rigours of starting out first as a junior doctor on hospital wards, then as a trainee general practitioner and finally as a partner in the practice and taking on responsibility for my own list of patients: not to mention marrying David and having and caring for two small children.

With this multitude of distractions, by 1989, I had been a doctor for fifteen years and had read almost no books not related directly to medicine, over the preceding twenty years at least. Then came the epiphany. The five partners in our practice in Kentish Town in London, where, in the end, I worked for nearly thirty-five years, decided to give each other a three-month sabbatical every ten years. We would be paid as normal and have no additional responsibilities other then returning refreshed and reinvigorated at the end of the three months. It was the equivalent of one extra week's holiday per year but the effect was transformative for all of us.

I decided to lie on the sofa and read books and I set about compiling a reading list. I included only two books relating to doctoring: the rereading of *A Fortunate Man* and Ian McWhinney's brilliant *Textbook of Family Medicine*[1] which I had been meaning to read for several years. Beyond these, I decided to dedicate myself to 'great novels' and, to help build my list, I wrote to a dozen or so people whose opinions I respected and asked them this: if you could read only ten novels in a lifetime, which ten would they be? (As I write this, I find myself deeply regretting not having asked John this same question when I had the chance.) Four novels appeared at some point in almost every list: *Anna Karenina*, *Emma*, *Bleak House*, and *Middlemarch*. Not surprisingly, given the lamentable state of my literary education, I had read none of them and it was such a delight to have the time to really relish them all for the first time when I was nearly forty. I immediately rediscovered the childhood joy of reading in the morning when I was rested, alert, and receptive and how different that reading is from the exhausted late-evening reading after work and chores are done.

Over the course of the three months, I made what was, for me, an extraordinary discovery as I slowly realized that reading novels

---

[1] McWhinney, I. *Textbook of Family Medicine*. Oxford University Press, 1981.

had as much to tell me about the work of general practice as any medical textbook.

In *Anna Karenina*, I read:

> Both of them now had only one thought—the illness … and the nearness of his death—which stifled all else. But neither of them dared speak of it, and so, whatever they said—without uttering the one thought that filled their minds—was all falsehood.

In *Emma:*

> It is very unfair to judge of anybody's conduct, without an intimate knowledge of their situation. Nobody, who has not been in the interior of a family, can say what the difficulties of any individual of that family may be.

In *Bleak House:*

> If I took my wrongs in any other way, I should be driven mad! It is only by resenting them, and by revenging them in my mind, and by angrily demanding the justice I never get, that I am able to keep my wits together.

And in *Middlemarch:*

> There is a forsaking which still sits at the same board and lies on the same couch with the forsaken soul, withering it the more by unloving proximity.

Each of these tiny excerpts had the miraculous power to summon up at least one of the many people that I had been attempting to care for as a general practitioner, and, in so doing, to broaden my sympathy and my understanding. I began to copy down any passage that resonated with my experience (and I still do). In the midst of the grotesque and self-harming idiocies of Brexit, I finally got around to reading *The Mill on the Floss* for the first time. I read this passage:

> It is easy enough to spoil the lives of our neighbours without taking so much trouble; we can do it by lazy acquiescence and lazy omission, by trivial falsities for which we hardly know a reason, by small frauds neutralised by small extravagances, by maladroit flatteries, and clumsily improvised insinuations.

And the extent to which George Eliot could have been writing about the evolving political situation 150 years later feels astounding.

Great novels have the capacity to capture the general in the particular, to write about the great sweeping and enduring truths of human life through the story of a particular individual in the full richness of their context, while holding both the general and the particular in balance. And this is just what the doctor must do: listen very carefully to the detail of the individual patient's experience and then draw on his or her knowledge of the generalizations of biomedical science and make a judgement as to whether any of these fits the patient's story and context well enough to offer the possibility of benefit, always remembering that each individual patient is different, each episode of illness is different and each manifestation of disease in a different person is different. And this is the reason why no treatments, including vaccines, should ever be mandated, except in the emergency of acute and dangerous psychosis.

Yet the miracle had its foundation in my rereading of *A Fortunate Man* which is, for me, the best book every written about general practice or family medicine and which would most certainly be on my list of ten books for a lifetime. Early on in the book John used his readings of Joseph Conrad to understand the process by which his Fortunate Man moved beyond his initial youthful prioritization of a fascination with dealing with life-and-death emergencies, which tends to make more mundane but no less vicious forms of suffering seem trivial and eventually resented, and replaced it with

> the intimation that the patient should be treated as a total person-
> ality, that illness is frequently a form of expression rather than a
> surrender to natural hazards.[2]

This was my first model of the power of literature to illuminate the world of practice at every level and this transformed my practice and led eventually to me wanting to write myself.

A lesser discovery was that, although the years of medical practice and the overwhelming volume of professional literature had developed my capacities for skimming and speed-reading research papers and newspapers in a dangerously superficial way, I have never tried to skim read a good novel because each word seems to matter, both demanding and rewarding proper attention. Similarly, each word spoken by a patient to a doctor also both demands and rewards and, in this way, reading novels taught me to pay real attention to words and to listen intently.

Of all the many wonderful books that I read during those three months, John's book was the only one that I was rereading and rereading is in itself an extraordinary experience. American critic and writer Wendy Lesser has written about reading the same

---

[2] Berger, J., and Mohr, J. *A Fortunate Man*. 1967. Penguin Books, 1969, p. 62.

book twice in a lifetime, as a younger and an older person.[3] She describes the dizzying effect of looking at a stationary work of art from two different points in time. The irreversibility of time means that the older reader is conscious of the younger one but the younger completely oblivious to the older and this asymmetry creates a sense of vertigo. So, while I was rereading *A Fortunate Man*, I was very conscious that my younger self had read the same words twenty years earlier but I could summon no recollection of my feelings and thoughts at the time, when I was a preclinical student only exposed to biomedical science. My only glimpse of a patient had been someone paraded at the front of a huge, raked lecture hall to demonstrate and exemplify some particular biomedical fact. I remember being discomfited by an approach which seemed to me to verge on exploitation. So, I knew nothing about how doctors and patients relate to each other and the ebb and flow of what goes on between them. Yet John's storytelling, combined with Jean Mohr's incredibly intimate photographs, is simultaneously so accessible and so profound that I read every word and I trust that some of its wisdom seeped into me and laid the foundation for the beginning of my own work with patients four years later. I am convinced that it must have reinforced my ambition to be a general practitioner caring for patients within their own communities, families, and homes and wearing their own clothes.

My older self marvelled at just how penetrating John's understanding of the work of general practice was. He eventually summarized it as

---

[3] Lesser, W. 'Sauntering through the Commas: The Pleasures of a Book Revisited'. *The Guardian*, Saturday 22 December 2001.

doing no more and no less than easing—and occasionally saving—
the lives of a few thousand of our contemporaries.[4]

And this is indeed the almost trivial but simultaneously gigantic
task which faces every working general practitioner. John was
able, having simply watched and listened over a period of six
weeks, to describe the most intimate and subtle of the interactions between doctor and patient. He did this in a way which was
completely familiar to those of us involved in this extraordinarily
privileged, yet always difficult work, but which is somehow lost
on almost all healthcare policymakers, most specialist colleagues
and even some general practitioners themselves. It is a book
which has inspired generations of doctors to have the courage
not only to look and to listen to their patients but to come close
enough to see and to hear.

By the time of this particular rereading, I was busy copying out
the phrases and sentences that felt particularly important to me
so I have a much clearer idea of how I reacted. I copied out no
fewer than 3,391 words, many of which I can now quote by heart,
and I know that this represents a much higher proportion than my
average.

Within the continuing relationships between doctors and
patients, and some of mine lasted the almost thirty-five years of
a professional lifetime, both parties are moving through time but
both carry a perception of their younger selves interacting with
the other and I find echoes of the same dizziness that is evoked by
rereading a book.

I found that, after my three months on the sofa, I had developed
a strange condition that means that I could now read almost

---

4 Berger, J., and Mohr, J. *A Fortunate Man*. 1967. Penguin Books, 1969, p. 165.

anything and find that it had some relevance to my work as a family doctor in general practice. This seemed almost another miracle and somehow must have to do with the fact that, under any system of universal healthcare provided free at the time of need, general practitioners have the privilege of seeing all sorts and conditions of people and feel themselves to be exposed to the whole of humanity. Any writing that explores the human condition has something to tell us.

After rereading *A Fortunate Man* again in 2014, I wrote to John:[5]

> I reread 'A Fortunate Man' and it reminded me of Richard Flanagan's marvellous novel 'Gould's Book of Fish':
>
>> Every time I opened the book a scrap of paper with some revelation I had not hitherto read would fall out, or I would stumble across an annotation that I had somehow missed in my previous readings, or I would come upon two pages stuck together that I hadn't noticed and which, when care-fully teased apart, would contain a new element of the story that would force me to rethink the whole in an entirely changed light.[6]
>
> This is what happens to me every time I read 'A Fortunate Man'—I find things that I have never noticed before—which I think is the sign of a really great book.
>
> This time I finally understood why Jean [Mohr]'s landscape photos are so important and the extent to which experience becomes imprinted on landscape—your line about the bend in the river reminding him of his failure. For me, of course, it is not a bend in a river, but a street corner or a particular block of flats or a front door. I understood how your use of Conrad demonstrates so clearly how great literature can be used to make sense of a life quite different from that depicted. I appreciated for the first time the

[5] 31 July 2014.
[6] Flanagan, R. *Gould's Book of Fish*. 2001. Picador, 2002, p. 28.

extraordinary prescience of your portrayal of emotional suffering causing 'physical' illness—which only now is being understood by most doctors. And finally, when I read that Sassall

> would subscribe to Goethe's dictum that 'Man knows him-self only inasmuch as he knows the world. He knows the world only within himself, and he is aware of himself only within the world. Each new object, truly recognized, opens a new organ within ourselves.'[7]

I realised that this passage is, at least in part, autobiographical. So— thank you once again for this my favourite book.

This was a very odd grammatical construction on my part and I think that with 'autobiographical' I was in fact referring to myself and trying to explain that rereading A Fortunate Man had served to open up a new organ of awareness within myself, which is cer-tainly what it felt like.

---

[7] Berger, J., and Mohr, J. A Fortunate Man. 1967. Penguin Books, 1969, p. 143.

PART TWO
IDEAS

4

COMMONPLACING

By the time I met John and we began to exchange letters I had already read many of his books and I had understood that the ideas and propositions in almost all of John's books resonated with my experience of my work as a general practitioner. The link was clearest for *A Fortunate Man* but the resonance spread far beyond that first introduction to his writing.

When thinking about the relationship between what I learned from reading his books and articles, and what I learned from our correspondence, I realize that from the beginning, I was corresponding with his books as much as with his person. My letters to him allowed me to draw in references from across his work and test out my understanding directly with the author, and he was then able to encourage me to look further and to go deeper.

I now understand that what we were doing together in our sequence of letters could be described as commonplacing. According to the *Oxford English Dictionary*, John Donne was one of the first to use this word and, in her 2022 biography of Donne, Katherine Rundell described:

> The practice of commonplacing—a way of seeking out and storing knowledge, so that you have multiple voices under a single heading—colours Donne's work; one thought reaches out to

Figure 3 Photograph by Iona Heath of books and a drawing by John Berger
Source: © John Berger and John Berger Estate.

another, across barriers of tradition, and ends up somewhere new and strange.

And:

Commonplacing plucks ideas out of their context and allows you to put them down against other, startling ones.[1]

So, in the succeeding pages, I will try to make this commonplacing explicit, drawing together what have been the ideas that have resonated most strongly for me from across John Berger's work and also from our correspondence; to put them down against each other, and bring multiple voices, from different times and

[1] Rundell, K. *Super-Infinite: The Transformations of John Donne.* 2022, pp. 36–39.

different places, under each single heading, with each thought reaching out to another to consolidate my learning and so try to illustrate the slow, iterative, and cumulative process which gradually deepened my understanding over all those years of reading.

5

THIS DOOR WHICH OPENS
ON TO WHAT?

The photo of the door by Jean Mohr, on which John Berger wrote his message for me more than twenty years ago, shows Dr Sassall either entering or leaving a room but what is quite clear is that he is engaged in visiting a patient in their own home. This is one of the burdens of general practice but also one of its great privileges, and even joys. I have entered a multitude of interiors, ranging from the elegant to the squalid, that I would never have had the opportunity to witness in a different sort of a life. The opening words of A Fortunate Man are:

> Sometimes a landscape seems to be less a setting for the life of its inhabitants than a curtain behind which their struggles, achievements and accidents take place.
> For those who, with the inhabitants are behind the curtain, landmarks are no longer only geographic but also biographical and personal.[1]

The patient's door is also a kind of curtain and the doctor in crossing its threshold moves in much the same way from the geographic to the biographical and personal. A patient seen in a consulting room can hide much that it is impossible to conceal within the intimacy of their own home. One learns so much:

[1] Berger, J., and Mohr, J. A Fortunate Man. 1967. Penguin Books, 1969, p. 13.

are there books, is the television on all the time, is there that pernicious smell of poverty or is everything just too perfect and spotless, are there toys, what do the pictures and photos on the walls show or suggest? I discovered that the sensation of sticking to the kitchen floor is most commonly associated with an old man living alone and not quite managing to cope after his wife has died. Once there was a gun on the table which was disconcerting in a council flat in inner-city London when, perhaps it would not have been in a remote country area. And I will never forget the moment when a glimpse of a tea towel decorated with a map of New Zealand and tacked to the wall helped me to understand much of the sadness and loneliness of the old lady standing in her impeccable kitchen.

In one of the essays included in his book *The Shape of the Pocket*, John wrote:

> And the slow process of discovering what is there without disturbing it, begins.[2]

And, immediately, I think that this is also what happens when I walk through the door into the room in which the patient has chosen to be seen; and beyond that, the words even begin to suggest the process of diagnosis itself. Yet the words were written as part of a correspondence with the artist Leon Kossoff to describe the process of drawing. The intention of the writer is not what I the reader find, peering through the lens of my own context. This is the miracle: the way in which the ordering of words in a single sentence can throw new light on an almost completely disconnected endeavour. And it is by this careful

[2] Berger, J. 'Drawing: Correspondence with Leon Kossoff'. In: Berger, J. *The Shape of the Pocket*. Bloomsbury, 2001, p. 80.

choice and ordering of words that reading John Berger helped me to understand my work more deeply and, I think and hope, to become better at it.

Later in the same correspondence with Kossoff, John described the 1638 portrait of *Aesop* by Velazquez, writing:

> He observes, watches, recognises, listens to what surrounds him and is exterior to him, and at the same time he ponders within, ceaselessly arranging what he has perceived, trying to find a sense which goes beyond the five senses with which he was born.[3]

And suddenly, with only a momentary hesitation over the gender-specific pronoun, I am back in the patient's room trying to bring all five of my senses to bear on the patient's predicament and their surroundings, human, physical, and cultural, and then filtering my perceptions through the framework of my biomedical knowledge: and so, trying to find my own sixth sense.

Through that door, photographed so skilfully by Jean Mohr, is at least one patient and, the sicker that patient feels, the more likely they are to be in or near a bed. In another essay in *The Shape of the Pocket*, John wrote about beds:

> Beds promise more than any other man-made object.
>
> ...
>
> The range of their promise is huge, from the modest to the voluptuous, from the timid to the ecstatic, from a pain's small relief to the great pain of happiness, from a little rest to death. ...
>
> Even a bed's smallest promise partakes of infinity ... Sleep.[4]

Before reading this, I had never really thought about my patients' beds but, as ever, John encourages me to pay attention. When I

[3] Berger, J. 'Drawing: Correspondence with Leon Kossoff'. In: Berger, J. *The Shape of the Pocket*. Bloomsbury, 2001, p. 82.
[4] Berger, J. 'Drawing: Correspondence with Leon Kossoff'. In: Berger, J. *The Shape of the Pocket*. Bloomsbury, 2001, p. 167.

do, I see a lot of modesty and timidity and, certainly, death either imminent or already achieved. Sometimes I can sense happiness but I have to imagine the voluptuous and the ecstatic and for some of the saddest and most damaged that imagining is difficult and too often close to impossible. Yet the very attempt to imagine the potential wonders of a bed makes me try to sense my patient's reality more deeply.

Some beds look comfortable and warm but too many do not. Most are reasonably clean in expectation of a doctor's visit but many are not and some are squalid and distressing for the patient and for me. Perhaps the most memorable bed of my career belonged to a sick old lady who lived alone and needed to be in hospital. She was very reluctant to go and the reason became clear when the ambulance staff arrived. The moment we lifted her out of bed, we realized that the copious bedding concealed a mass of bank notes! It was not the moment to ask and, sadly, I never did discover the story behind them.

In a letter to John,[5] I asked:

> Did I tell you that I have found a wonderful new word? It is Icelandic—*nær-gætni*—and apparently it means near-carefulness—the care that needs to be taken when one comes near to another. I can't think of anything equivalent in English and I wonder what makes words appear in one language and not in another. It's a word for me to think a lot about and to try to work with.

I wrote this because I knew that, without knowing the word, John had written about its meaning on many occasions, all of them relevant to the attitude of the doctor as he or she walks through the door.

[5] 17 August 2005.

In the last story in *Once in Europa* which is titled 'Play Me Something', John wrote:

> She liked the way he hesitated before speaking, it was very deliberate, as if each time he answered one of her questions, he came to the door of a house, opened it to a visitor, and then spoke.[6]

And I think of the gentleness with which we must ask important, intimate questions of the sick, the fearful, the timid, and the old, which, I hope, is why I didn't question my patient about the banknotes in her bed.

In the story 'Stones' in the book *Hold Everything Dear: Dispatches on Survival and Resistance*, John described:

> An expression of great attention to the moment. Calm and considered, as if it could conceivably be the last moment.[7]

He was writing about a young money-changer in Palestine who sought him out in the vegetable market after discovering that he had given John fifty shekels too little. Their interaction appears to have nothing to do with the care of a patient in their own home but, once again, here is the magic. As they come through the door, every seriously committed doctor needs just this expression of great attention to the moment because it is the stuff of *nær-gætni*. The challenge of attention and its great advocate Simone Weil became a central part of our correspondence and, whenever I write now, it is John's extraordinary drawing of Simone Weil that looks down on me:

[6] Berger, J. *Once in Europa*. Vintage International, 1992, p. 157.
[7] Berger, J. *Hold Everything Dear: Dispatches on Survival and Resistance*. Verso, 2007, p. 72.

Figure 4 Portrait of Simone Weil by John Berger
Source: © John Berger and John Berger Estate.

John had written to me[8] about his discovery of the lumi-
nous essays written by Kathleen Jamie, the Scottish poet
who was appointed as the Makar, the Scottish National Poet,
in 2021.[9]

I replied,[10] linking Weil and Jamie:

> I came across two passages from Czesław Miłosz—both of which
> made me think of you. The first was a tiny quotation at the end of
> his essay on Simone Weil.[11] He writes:
>
>> Her intelligence, the precision of her style were nothing but
>> a very high degree of attention to the sufferings of mankind.
>> And, as she says, 'Absolutely unmixed attention is prayer.'
>
> And 'absolutely unmixed attention' seems to me to be exactly what
> Kathleen Jamie attempts. And I think it is also what I try to teach
> medical students.

And, of course, what John had been trying to teach me all along.

---

[8] 3 February 2006.
[9] https://literaturealliancescotland.co.uk/kathleen-jamie-appointed-as-scotlands-new-makar/
[10] 29 May 2006.
[11] Miłosz, C. 'The Importance of Simone Weil'. In: *To Begin Where I Am: Selected Essays.* New York: Farrar, Strauss and Giroux, 2001 p. 259.

6

LOOKING

L ooking at a newspaper photograph, John tried to describe
every particular, visible or imaginable: the way her hair is parted,
her bruised cheek, her slightly swollen lower lip, her name and
all the different significations it has acquired according to who is
addressing her, memories of her own childhood, the individual
quality of her hatred of her interrogator, the gifts she was born
with, every detail of the circumstances under which she has so far
escaped death, the intonation she gives to the name of each person
she loves, the diagnosis of whatever medical weaknesses she may
have and their social and economic causes, everything that she
opposes in her subtle mind to the muzzle of the gun jammed
against her temple.[1]

The photograph shows a South Vietnamese peasant being interro-
gated by an American soldier. It is a horrific image but, in describing it, John set a standard for observation and empathic imagination that, as a doctor, I need to try to emulate. If I look carefully, I
will begin to perceive the story of a life.

In his essay 'Modigliani's Alphabet of Love',[2] moving from looking at photographs to looking at paintings, John wrote:

---

[1] Berger, J. *Selected Essays and Articles: The Look of Things*. Penguin Books, 1972, p. 51.
[2] Berger, J. 'Modigliani's Alphabet of Love'. In: *The Sense of Sight*. Vintage International,
1985, p. 104.

Only by considering a painting's method, the practice of its transformation, can we be confident about the direction of its image, the direction of the image's passage towards us and past us. Every painting comes from far away (many fail to reach us), yet we only receive a painting fully if we are looking in the direction from which it has come. This is why seeing a painting is so different from seeing an object.

But, as I discovered, not so different from looking at a person. By teaching me how to look at a painting (and I have been fascinated by Modigliani ever since I read this essay), John gives me very important clues about how to look at a person. Many patients come from far away, some physically, some emotionally, some culturally, and many fail to reach us as we struggle to reach across the barriers erected by very different life experiences. Yet this notion of the direction of gaze helps us to take more account of these barriers and to strive to look in the direction from which he or she has come. Looking at paintings becomes useful practice for thoughtful looking at patients.

In 'The Moment of Cubism', another essay included in his book *The Sense of Sight*, John took this further:

> In a Cubist picture, the conclusion and the connections are given. They are what the picture is made of. They are its content. The spectator has to find his place within this content whilst the complexity of the forms and the 'discontinuity' of the space remind him that his view from that place is bound to be only partial.
>
> Such content and its functioning was prophetic because it coincided with the new scientific view of nature which rejected simple causality and the single permanent all-seeing viewpoint.[3]

---

[3] Berger, J. 'The Moment of Cubism'. In: *The Sense of Sight*. Vintage International, 1985, p. 180.

Regrettably, medicine has been rather slow to reject simple causality and is still far too keen on assuming a single permanent all-seeing viewpoint, while simply ignoring aspects of the patient's body or mind or experience that do not fit. This was very nicely demonstrated by the work of Gene Feder's team observing Rapid Access Chest Pain clinics:[4]

> We found that patients rarely gave a history that, without further interrogation, satisfied the doctors, who actively restructured the complex narrative until it fitted a diagnostic canon, detaching it from the patient's interpretation and explanation.

Significant chunks of the patient's narrative seemed to be discounted in order to fit, or not, diagnostic criteria. This is not only dangerous but betrays a lack of interest, not only in the person of the patient but also in the possibility of the patient's story including a clue to new knowledge.

I am reminded of my favourite 'Memorable patient' article from the British Medical Journal, submitted by a general practitioner in 1997.[5] The doctor had been summarizing his patients' records and had discovered the record of a consultation from ten years earlier that he remembered very well. The patient had come for a repeat prescription of antibiotics for his acne rosacea and mentioned in passing that the antibiotics helped his indigestion. He made a note: 'Occ. Indigestion. Says oxytet cures it!' Ten years later, he reflected that 'the patient may seem peculiar, but he may be telling you something that is revolutionary. We ignore such things that do not fit into the standard view at our peril.' In the preceding

---

[4] Somerville, C., Featherstone, K., Hemingway, H., Timmis, A., and Feder, G. 'Performing Stable Angina Pectoris: An Ethnographic Study'. *Social Science & Medicine*. 2008, 66: 1497e1508.

[5] Roscoe, T. 'A Memorable Patient: Early Treatment of H Pylori'. *BMJ*. 1997, 315(7101): 315.

years, how many other doctors heard patients making similar remarks and discounted them as irrelevant, so passing up any possibility of beating Barry J. Marshall and J. Robin Warren to the discovery of the infectious agent *Helicobacter pylori* and the subsequent Nobel Prize for Medicine in 2005.

In the same 'Moment of Cubism' essay, John went on to quote from the German theoretical physicist and Nobel laureate, Weiner Heisenberg, in his 1959 book *Physics and Philosophy*:

> One may say that the human ability to understand may be in a certain sense unlimited. But the existing scientific concepts cover always only a very limited part of reality, and the other part that has not yet been understood is infinite. Whenever we proceed from the known to the unknown we may hope to understand, but we may have to learn at the same time a new meaning of the word understanding.

And he drew a parallel between the partial viewpoint in a Cubist painting and the very real limits of human understanding, all of which urges more diffidence, more humility, and more doubt in the practice of medicine.

Perhaps beginning to worry about a lack of diffidence among some curators of art exhibitions, I wrote[6] to John:

> A few weeks ago, I went to visit a patient—a man who lives alone in a bedsit and who looks very much older than his sixty-something years. He had been in and out of hospital because of the effects of continually combining his medication with considerable amounts of alcohol. For once, he was sober and we were able to talk about the paintings on the walls of his room— his own paintings—dark sombre views of the canal and the streets—detailed, careful likenesses—but imagined as well as recorded.

[6] 22 January 2006.

Yesterday, I went to see the Tate Modern exhibition of Henri Rousseau and I was reminded of the quiet determination of my patient's paintings. Some of Rousseau's paintings are very familiar but many I had never seen before and the more I looked, the stranger it felt. And then I found myself thinking—first about Joseph Conrad and then about Kipling's *Jungle Book* and *Just-So Stories*—and it seemed to me that all that deep disturbing colonialist guilt is in the Rousseau paintings—he seems to raise all the questions that are in *Heart of Darkness* and—like Conrad—leaves the questions all intact with no consoling answers. And the gallery was full of children and this seemed to underline a conventional view that because his paintings are naïve (whatever that really means) they are somehow easy—but they seemed to me to be anything but. The gallery interpretation presented Rousseau as someone who created an exotic world from his careful studies in the Jardin des Plantes and at the 1889 World's Fair but I find it hard to believe that he was genuinely as naïve as this appears to suggest and that he had no notion of the disturbing questions that I find in his paintings now. The handout says: 'He would have been enthralled by the mock tribal villages whose inhabitants had been shipped in from French colonies around the world to recreate life in West Africa, or the East Indies, or Indochina as a tourist display in the heart of Paris.' I see something but it doesn't look or feel like 'enthralled'.

His cheering reply came ten days later[7]:

Iona—You're right, I think. 'Enthralled! ...' my arse! It seems more likely that he, dubbed as a 'primitive', might have felt intensely the destruction, the loss, being suffered by others, dubbed in a different context, 'primitive'. . . . his paintings are (surely?) about a vision concerning 'the soul' of things—souls which were being denied and destroyed by the positivism of the new colonialism—as observed by Conrad, and which is there as a ghost in Kipling.

And I felt that I was slowly learning to look.

---

[7] 3 February 2006.

7

SEEING

Looking and seeing are very different: it is impossible to see without looking but all too easy to look without seeing. Looking is often quite passive but seeing demands engagement and attention. Looking can, and perhaps mostly does, occur at a distance but you need to get close to someone to see them. Doctors have to learn to move from looking to seeing and to achieve this they have to have the courage to get close enough. John taught me to look but perhaps more than anything his writing taught me to try to really see.

In an essay entitled *Drawings by Watteau*, he wrote:

> An artist's observation is not just a question of his using his eyes; it is the result of his honesty, of his fighting with himself to understand what he sees.[1]

And, reading this, it is completely impossible for me not to think of my work as a doctor and how I too must fight, every working day, to understand what I see, to use my experience and my imagination to move beyond my initial superficial impression; to fight with myself because perhaps the greatest barrier to understanding is, almost always, the assumption that one knows the answer already.

[1] Berger, J. *Selected Essays and Articles: The Look of Things.* Penguin Books, 1972, p. 104.

In his 1980 essay on *The Eyes of Claude Monet* he wrote:

> Given the precision and the vagueness you are forced to re-see the
> lilacs of your own experience. The precision triggers your visual
> memory, while the vagueness welcomes and accommodates your
> memory when it comes.[2]

So, I am looking at Monet's beautiful purple lilacs and, miracu-
lously, they are both precise and vague. These are not necessarily
simple opposites but the words combine to moderate each
other rather than being static and separate. Yet the juxtaposition
is momentarily startling and evokes other familiar contrasts:
between the general and the particular, or between doubt and
certainty. Perhaps when I am looking at a patient, I need to try to
see both the precision and the vagueness, both what is unique to
that particular patient and, at the same time, what evokes memories of other patients which might help me to discover what is
happening to them. Vagueness evokes the sweeping generalizations so common in medicine, politics, and life; precision pays
attention to the detail of life and experience. To see, I need to look
both deeply and broadly. And, of course, I never look at lilacs in
quite the same way again.

In *A Fortunate Man: The Story of a Country Doctor*, John was clearly
both looking and seeing as he observed the practice of his friend
John Sassall, and he wrote a great deal about the necessity and
challenge of recognition:

> He is acknowledged as a good doctor because he meets the deep
> and unformulated expectation of the sick for a sense of fraternity.
> He recognizes them. Sometimes he fails . . . but there is about him
> the constant will of a man trying to recognize.[3]

---

[2] Berger, J. 'The Eyes of Claude Monet'. In: *The Sense of Sight*. 1985. Vintage International,
1993, p. 193.
[3] Berger, J., and Mohr, J. *A Fortunate Man*. 1967. Penguin Books, 1969, p. 76.

It is far too easy to fail especially when overworked and under-staffed and struggling to care for a local population which finds itself on the losing side of almost every political and policy innova-tion and becoming ever more damaged by the structural violence of an increasingly polarized and unequal society. Nonetheless the constant effort of will remains essential and, so often, in and of itself, makes a tangible difference to patient and doctor alike:

> An unhappy patient comes to a doctor to offer him an illness—in the hope that this part of him at least (the illness) may be recogniz-able.... If the man can begin to feel recognized—and such recogni-tion may well include aspects of his character which he has not yet recognized himself—the hopeless nature of his unhappiness will have been changed: he may even have the chance of being happy.[4]

When I read and reread this extraordinary book, one of its great gifts is that I myself feel recognized in the work that I try to do and so I understand the power that recognition carries to help a patient feel less vulnerable and less alone. Making a correct biomedical diagnosis can be an important part of that recognition but under-standing and acknowledgement of the story of at least part of a life is what builds the trust between patient and doctor that enables treatment and ongoing careful care.

In his 1987 book *Stories of Sickness*, American bioethicist and fam-ily physician Howard Brody elaborated on John's understanding in *A Fortunate Man*, of the vital importance of explicitly recogniz-ing suffering. Brody uses this understanding to explore Sophocles' story of Philoctetes[5] and his stinking wound. Odysseus has abandoned Philoctetes on the island of Lemnos ten years before but now he realizes that the Greeks cannot win the Trojan War

4 Berger, J., and Mohr, J. *A Fortunate Man*. 1967. Penguin Books, 1969, p. 75.
5 Heaney, S. *The Cure at Troy*. Faber & Faber, 1990.

without Philoctetes's bow. Odysseus takes Achilles' son Neoptolemus with him and plans to use the boy to trick Philoctetes into giving up his bow. Odysseus's approach is entirely instrumental whereas Neoptolemus sees the extent of Philoctetes's suffering and responds to it so that, as Brody wrote:

> In the terminology of Berger, Neoptolemus has performed the vital function of recognizing Philoctetes in his suffering and anguish, and thus has engaged in the crucial social role of restoring Philoctetes to a sense of full personhood.[6]
>
> ...
>
> Odysseus realizes that we rob the sick of their social power over us if we somehow suppress the human reaction to their plight. But Neoptolemus (speaking for Sophocles) realizes that there is another way to turn aside the power of the sick person, when that power is directed toward continued suffering and bitterness instead of toward healing; and that is the route of re-establishing fully human contact so as to graphically remind the sick person of the importance of social connectedness. The sick person may indeed have accepted solitude as preferable to being rebuffed in his search for sympathy, and may have tried hard to forget about the importance of social relationships in maintaining identity and self-respect. But Sophocles argues that these are only temporary barriers that cannot withstand the concerted efforts of the reaching out of human sympathy.

Sophocles pays tribute to the power of recognition in the care of those who are suffering. What John saw and what Jean Mohr photographed in that country practice in the Forest of Dean had been known for millennia but its importance is still not understood by many of those caring for patients today.

---

[6] Brody, H. *Stories of Sickness*. Yale University Press, 1987, p. 125.

45

In his essay *Erasing the Past,* John argued that:

> Appearances like words can also be read and, amongst appearances, the human face constitutes one of the longest texts.[7]

And, in his essay *Manhattan,* John described the extent to which:

> The traces left by experience on a person's face are the traces of meetings (or struggles) between the person's inner needs or intentions and the demands or offers of the outside world. Put differently: marks of experience on a face are the lines of conjuncture between two moulds; both moulds are social products, but one contains a self and the other history.[8]

He was challenging us all to see faces and imagine the stories they might have lived, and never to be satisfied with a quick glance. He encourages a doctor to ask gentle hesitant questions about the individual experience of inner needs and their possible conflict with the harshness of the outside world. Perhaps the most powerful examples are the faces of the homeless who almost always look older than their years due not only to the unforgiving nature of life on the streets but also to the miserable childhood and later life experiences that have so often led, eventually, to their becoming homeless.

I wrote to John:[9]

> Last week, we went to see Arthur Miller's *Death of a Salesman.* I had never seen it before and so I had never heard Linda Loman's speech about her husband and the imperative of attention:
> 'I don't say he's a great man.
> Willy Loman never made a lot of money. His name was never in the paper. He's not the finest character that ever lived. But he's a

[7] https://www.spokesmanbooks.com/Spokesman/PDF/97Berger.pdf
[8] Berger J. 'Manhattan'. In: *The Sense of Sight.* 1985. Vintage International, 1993, p. 64.
[9] 30 June 2005.

human being, and a terrible thing is happening to him. So attention must be paid. He's not to be allowed to fall into his grave like an old dog.

Attention, attention must be finally paid to such a person.'

In the play, Willy Loman's inner needs were most certainly being battered by the rigours of his world.

In his essay, *The Sight of a Man,* John wrote about the achievement of Cezanne:

He [Cézanne] testified that the visibility of things belongs to each one of us: not in so far as our minds interpret signals received by our eyes; but in so far as the visibility of things is our recognition of them.[10]

In his Booker prize-winning novel *G.,* he again invokes Cezanne: 'One minute in the life of the world is going by. Paint it as it is.'[11]

For anyone who does not paint, the injunction becomes 'See it as it is'. Or at the very least, try to.

Thinking about the art of Jackson Pollock in his essay *A Kind of Sharing,* John wrote about Pollock's deliberate negation of the act of faith that had remained a constant throughout the history of art:

The act of faith consisted of believing that the visible contained hidden secrets, that to study the visible was to learn something more than could be seen in a glance. Thus, paintings were there to reveal a presence behind an appearance—be it that of a Madonna, a tree or, simply, the light that soaks through a red.[12]

[10] Berger, J. 'The Sight of a Man'. In: *Selected Essays and Articles: The Look of Things.* Penguin Books, 1972, p. 197.
[11] Berger, J. *G.* 1972. Bloomsbury Publishing, 1996, p. 15.
[12] Berger, J. 'A Kind of Sharing'. In: *Keeping a Rendezvous.* 1985. Vintage International, 1993, p. 115.

Figure 5 Sketch of the author by John Berger

Source: © John Berger and John Berger Estate.

Note: John's drawing of me in the garden in Quincy, 21 July 2013, with small blotches as it began to rain.

Really seeing is learning something more than can be caught in a glance and perhaps it has been a constant in the history of medicine too. Yet I fear with our increasing faith in the sort of seeing that is done by machines, this approach is being undermined.

In 'A Professional Secret', John described the intensity of looking required for its action to be transformed into seeing:

> If one thinks of appearances as a frontier, one might say that painters search for messages which cross the frontier: messages which come back from the visible.
>
> ...
>
> To draw is not only to measure and put down, it is also to receive. When the intensity of looking reaches a certain degree, one becomes aware of an equally intense energy coming towards one, through the appearance of whatever it is one is scrutinizing.[13]

This reciprocation seems fair enough but, for a doctor, it can take courage to submit to scrutiny and any flinching can disrupt an entire consultation. For me, the marker of flinching is an inability to look someone in the eye and an inappropriate diffidence which seems to make it impossible to say something which I know needs to be said.

I wrote[14] to John about an exhibition of the sculpture of his friend Juan Muñoz who had died suddenly and unexpectedly while his *Double Bind* installation in the Tate Modern Turbine Hall was still on show:

[13] Berger, J. 'A Professional Secret'. In: *Keeping a Rendezvous*. 1985. Vintage International, 1993, p. 115.
[14] 7 January 2002.

We keep being drawn back to see the Juan Muñoz at the Tate Modern—it seems to be about so many things—about hidden places and hidden people in cities—about taking things for granted—about not caring about the people you don't see—about what goes on behind faces—about lives that intersect and lives that just pass by. And now of course it is also about loss—and how art changes when the artist has died.

Sometimes it feels that the doctors in general practice are put there to care about the people that the rich and powerful don't see and don't want to see. What we learn is just how much courage, endurance, and even wonder, they miss by choosing not to see.

8

LISTENING

In 1985, the Arts Council of Great Britain curated a touring exhibition of the *Pilgrims* photographs of Markéta Luskačová. Trying to imagine how he might describe the photographs to someone who could not see them, John wrote in the tiny postcard-sized catalogue:

> Appearances and words speak so differently; the visual never allows itself to be translated intact into the verbal.[1]

These are words to be taken seriously because they come from someone much of whose life's work was to attempt this impossible task of translation. They tell the doctor in me that neither looking/seeing nor listening/hearing are ever sufficient in themselves when trying to understand a patient's situation, story, and sickness. Both have to be done consciously and deliberately: looking carefully in order to see and listening carefully in order to hear—each speaks differently and reveals different things. We often say to students and young doctors, 'Don't interrupt, just shut up and listen.' Perhaps we should add, 'But don't stop looking and trying to see.'

I was lucky enough to be taught to shut up and listen by a patient who had been exposed to almost every possible dimension of

[1] Berger, J. Text for *Markéta Luskačová: Pilgrims*. Arts Council of Great Britain, 1985.

disadvantage and had been abused and damaged by them. Yet she was the most effective teacher. Somehow, she exemplified John's description in his novel *Lilac and Flag*:

> People say that bodies reveal character. They are wrong. Bodies are dealt out to us like cards. Character begins with how you play what you get.[2]

She would come into my consulting room and start to tell me the story of what was happening and, if I had the temerity to interrupt, she would simply pause, take a breath, and start the story again from the beginning. I learnt quickly that I should keep quiet.

In his 2005 book, *Here Is Where we Meet*, John described walking into the Ritz Hotel in Madrid:

> As soon as one comes off the street and the double glass doors swing shut, one is aware here of the deafness of money, which, like the depth of the ocean, is perceived not as an empty silence, but as a seclusion.[3]

Unlike the poor, the rich are not obliged to listen to what they do not want to hear, but perhaps this seclusion also excludes them from much that they need to hear or in which they might even find connection, interest, and even joy.

In *Hold Everything Dear: Dispatches on Survival and Resistance*, John ventured:

> Democracy is a proposal (rarely realized) about decision making; it has little to do with election campaigns. Its promise is that political decisions be made after, and in the light of, consultation with the governed. This is dependent upon the governed being adequately

---

[2] Berger, J. *Lilac and Flag*. 1992. Vintage International, 1999, p. 6.
[3] Berger, J. *Here Is Where We Meet*. Bloomsbury Publishing, 2005, p. 143.

informed about the issues in question, and upon decision-makers having the capacity and will to listen and take account of what they have heard. Democracy should not be confused with the 'freedom' of binary choices, the publication of opinion polls or the crowding of people into statistics. These are its pretences.[4]

Taken together, these go some way to explain the impotent fury I feel in the face of the careless and self-interested exercise of power across the world today. With remarkably few exceptions, those with power or money (and how often these are aligned) seek out and welcome their seclusion and have no will to listen and to take account of what they have heard. The greater the power or money, the less willingness to listen. Yet every working day, alongside general practitioners up and down the country (and indeed the world) I have listened intently to patients' stories which all too often lay bare the structural violence let loose by the abuse of power and money, and describe in detail exactly how policy plays out in the ordinary lives of ordinary people. Very few people enjoy the privilege of listening to these stories and almost no one in government wants to listen to us when we bring reports from the frontline of primary care medicine. Again, John had it precisely: 'Reality is inimical to those with power.'[5]

I wrote[6] to John:

Could I try something else out on you? I have been reading about a philosopher, called Gadamer, of whom I know nothing except that he wrote about 'the infinity of the unsaid'. The paper[7] in which

[4] Berger, J. Hold Everything Dear: Dispatches on Survival and Resistance. Verso, 2007, p. 41.
[5] Berger, J. And Our Faces, My Heart, Brief as Photos. 1984. Vintage International, 1991, p. 73.
[6] 26 March 2000.
[7] Anderson, H., and Goolishian, H. A. 'Human Systems as Linguistic Systems: Preliminary and Evolving Ideas about the Implications for Clinical Theory'. Family Process. 1988, 27: 371–393.

this was mentioned is about stories and narrative—and about how the stories of those who are mentally ill have been distorted and coerced by social and political pressure, and by abuse and trauma, but that every story is surrounded by 'the infinity of the unsaid'. Life is so rich and complex that every strand of any story simplifies and focuses on one part (like a photograph? Or like your patterns of stars in the night sky?)[8] and there are always many different stories that could be told. And that part of listening can be to try and help to find and to hear a different, hidden story that is not so stereotyped by the labels inflicted by the conventions of society and psychiatry. Does that make any sense? I am more and more convinced that the diagnostic labels used by psychiatry are almost completely useless.

I seem to be groping towards the idea that just by listening and responding gently and thoughtfully I could begin to help my patients to tell slightly different stories; ones which revealed more of their undoubted reserves of courage and endurance in often appalling circumstances, and stories which would somehow lessen their burden of shame and allow them greater stature and presence.

Also, in *And Our Faces*, John wrote:

> Those who read or listen to our stories see everything as through a lens. This lens is the secret of narration, and it is ground anew in every story, ground between the temporal and the timeless.[9]

Listening through a lens is an odd metaphor, but, thinking it through, it helps me to find those different stories by trying to grind a different lens so that I can hear beneath the immediate story the more profound and less destructive one.

---

[8] Berger, J. *And Our Faces, My Heart, Brief as Photos*. 1984. Vintage International, 1991, p. 8.
[9] Berger, J. *And Our Faces, My Heart, Brief as Photos*. 1984. Vintage International, 1991, p. 31.

9

CONNECTING

How do doctors and patients connect and begin to open up the lines of communication between them and to understand and trust each other? It usually begins with question and answer but must move rapidly beyond the standardized rituals of the consultation.

In the book *Hold Everything Dear*, in his essay about the appalling aftermath of Hurricane Katrina, John wrote:

> Sometimes it happens that a question is for a moment more pertinent than answers or explanations.[1]

And I was sure that Anton Chekhov had written something similar. I checked and it was in a letter to Alexei Suvorin:

> You confuse two things, solving a problem and stating a problem correctly. It is only the second that is obligatory for the artist.[2]

Chekhov was, of course, a doctor as well as a consummate artist so he will have known that the second is also obligatory for the doctor. Premature attempts at providing answers can be dangerous and destructive. Only if the problem is stated correctly does any possibility of solving it arise, and then only by looking and seeing and listening and hearing, and slowly formulating,

---

[1] Berger, J. *Hold Everything Dear: Dispatches on Survival and Resistance.* Verso, 2007, p. 107.
[2] Bamforth, I. *A Doctor's Dictionary: Writings on Culture and Medicine.* Carcanet, 2015, p. 93.

and then an iteration of asking and checking the doctor's under-standing against the patient's experience of his or her symptoms. Asking always requires that delicate combination of courage and gentleness which is fundamental not only to effective practice but also to all John's writing.

John wrote[3] to me:

> Meanwhile I need to talk to you. Not urgent. Any time in the next week when you have (what utopianism) a half hour to spare! It's not about my health, but about how to deal with somebody else who is in trouble—and before which trouble I find myself more and more lost.
>
> I know that even you can do nothing really. But I have a hunch that just talking to you, or, more, listening to you, might offer me a hand—and it seems to me I've lost both mine.

He was not asking for answers he was asking for a conversation, for the opportunity to talk and to listen.

A few weeks later, he wrote[4] again:

> Don't worry. I'm OK. I got lost trying to save someone from being lost. It's better now. If it's bad again, I'll appeal to you.

John made drawings all his life and, in his book *Bento's Sketchbook*, he describes four drawings he made of Subcomandante Marcos in the Chiapas, south-east Mexico around Christmas 2007:

> Maybe the four are not proper drawings but simply sketch maps of an encounter. Maps that make it less likely to get lost. A question of hope.[5]

In any meeting between a doctor and a patient, the doctor needs to have similar sketch map in mind, in order not to get lost and to

---

[3] 12 May 2002.
[4] 11 June 2002.
[5] Berger, J. *Bento's Sketchbook*. Pantheon Books, 2011, p. 10.

hold onto hope of being in some sense useful to the patient. The map will usually show a sequence of the tentative stages that I have been describing and will include looking, listening, asking, touching, and finding the right words in which to state the problem.

Describing Dr Sassall in *A Fortunate Man*, John wrote:

> He is continually being reminded of how much difference a moment can make and of how irreversible, how carefully prepared the process which leads up to that moment is.[6]

Part of the secret is to be acutely aware of moments without thinking about the pressure of time—or, worse still, looking at the clock or a watch. In those special consultations when one might be lured into thinking that one had become quite good at the job, there is almost always a crucial moment around which everything turns. Equally there are pivotal moments where things begin to go badly wrong and any hope of mutual understanding and effective communication is completely undermined.

In *Here Is Where We Meet*, John invoked the essential notion of style: essential not only to the art of living but also to the art of medical practice:

> Style? A certain lightness. A sense of shame excluding certain actions or reactions. A certain proposition of elegance. The supposition that, despite everything, a melody can be looked for and sometimes found. … Style is about an invisible promise. This is why it requires and encourages a talent for endurance and an ease with time. Style is very close to music.[7]

At the same time, John is illustrating his own style of writing and thinking. Each line of this paragraph could almost be a line of

---

[6] Berger, J., and Mohr, J. *A Fortunate Man*. 1967. Penguin Books, 1969, p. 126.
[7] Berger, J. *Here Is Where We Meet*. Bloomsbury Publishing, 2005, p. 168.

poetry and, just like a poem, the immediate meaning of the words seems to reverberate with something deeper. In a sense it could be described as solo commonplacing; each thought reaches out to another, and ends up somewhere new, creating the potential for new thoughts. The secret of both poetry and commonplacing is that the reader is not told what to think but is challenged to participate in this process of discovering new connections and new ideas.

Perhaps, it is style that gives any good conversation a certain lightness and elegance and the same applies to a good consultation within which both doctor and patient are able to sense its elegance. And every doctor needs to have their talent for endurance and ease with time encouraged. Sadly, the vast majority of health service policymakers have no understanding of this need, the fulfilment of which brings the hard-pressed (and rarely thanked) the joy, reward, and motivation of a job well done. In his magnificent, campaigning book, *Why We Revolt*, the Peruvian-American physician Victor Montori also emphasized a certain proposition of elegance:

> The elegance of a thoughtful practice. Taking their time, more deliberate toil than mad rush, to improve their craft.
> …
> Caring is not meant to be efficient, it is meant to be elegant.[8]

In *The Look of Things*, John seemed to touch on imagination as a component of elegance and on the impossibility of using it as a bureaucratic metric.:

> The effectiveness of a work of imagination cannot be estimated quantitatively. Its performance is not isolatable or repeatable. It changes with circumstances. It creates its own situation. There is

[8] Montori, V. *Why We Revolt: A Patient Revolution for Careful and Kind Care*. Mayo Clinic Press, 2017, pp. 70–71.

no foreseeable quantitative correlation between the quality of a work of imagination and its effectiveness. And this is part of its nature because it is intended to operate within a field of subjective interactions which are interminable and immeasurable.[9]

General practitioners can only work within a field of subjective interactions, their own and their patient's, and John argued that the nature of these interactions is to be interminable and immeasurable, both of which qualities are an anathema to the bureaucratic mind. In this context, perhaps we should be less surprised by the extent to which the continuity of care within healthcare in general and primary healthcare in particular, has been deliberately undermined over several decades by the industrialization of healthcare. My friend John Nessa, the philosopher prince of my generation of general practitioners in Norway, pointed out an obvious truth that I had never recognized until he said that a tenth conversation between two individuals is necessarily different from the first, because both individuals have been changed by the previous interactions over time. The patient's account of their situation and the doctor's questions will be different.

In 2019, I was lucky enough to attend a workshop at a family medicine conference in Kyoto in Japan, run by family medicine trainees and designed to demonstrate the relevance of traditional Japanese culture to the teaching of family medicine. The traditional activities included flower arranging and judo but, for me the most striking was the tea ceremony and some beautiful, related calligraphy. One of the young doctors had created a banner with the Japanese characters that spell out 'Ichi-go Ichi-e' which, we were told, means 'One life, One meeting'.

---

[9] Berger, J. *Selected Essays and Articles: The Look of Things*. Penguin Books, 1972, p. 188.

Figure 6 Japanese calligraphy

They explained that no tea ceremony can be the same even if both participants are the same people because both are changing over time and the trainees argued that this is just the same for consultations. All this underlines the importance of continuity of care[10] and there has been recent scientific, quantitative research which confirms that patients receiving continuing care from an individual doctor live longer and have less premature disease.[11]

In spring 2005, Gareth Evans conceived and curated *Here Is Where We Meet*, a magnificent six-week John Berger season across London, which celebrated every aspect of his work and coincided with the publication of the book with the same title. There was a showing of the 1989 film for the BBC, *Another Way of Telling: Views of Photography*, a collaboration between John Berger and Jean Mohr, photographed and directed by John Christie. I wrote[12] to John Berger about the film:

> The moment in *Another Way of Telling* when you talk about putting still photographs into a sequence and how the one before influences how we see the one that comes after—and this is absolutely true for still photographs—how much more must it be true for conversations between people and yet we seem to have a government and policy-makers who think that health care can be delivered without any continuity—with the patient seeing a

[10] Pereira Gray, D. J., Sidaway-Lee, K., White, E. et al. 'Continuity of Care with Doctors—a Matter of Life and death? A Systematic Review of Continuity of Care and Mortality'. *BMJ Open*. 2018, 8: e021161. doi: 10.1136/bmjopen-2017-021161

[11] Sandvik, H., Hetlevik, Ø., Blinkenberg, J., and Hunskaar, S. 'Continuity in General Practice as Predictor of Mortality, Acute Hospitalisation, and Use of Out-of-Hours Care: A Registry-based Observational Study in Norway'. *British Journal of General Practice*. 2022, 72(715): e84–e90. doi: 10.3399/BJGP.2021.0340. PMID: 34607797; PMCID: PMC8510690

[12] 12 May 2005.

different doctor on each occasion that they need care. I come close to despair—and then after writing this, I find where you have written: 'Despair is the emotion which follows a sense of betrayal.'[13]

And how true that is.

---

[13] Berger, J. Dispatches: Undefeated Despair. *Race & Class.* 2006, 48(1): 31.

10

TOUCHING

Discussing Modigliani's highly distinctive portraits in his essay 'Modigliani's Alphabet of Love', John wrote:

> Everything begins with the skin, the flesh, the surface of that body, the envelope of that soul. Whether the body is naked or clothed, whether the extent of that skin is finally bordered by a fringe of hair, by a neckline of a dress, or by a contour of a torso or a flank, makes little difference. Whether the body is male or female makes no difference. All that makes a difference is whether the painter had, or had not, crossed that frontier of imaginary intimacy on the far side of which a vertiginous tenderness begins. Everything begins with the skin and what outlines it. And everything is completed there too. Along that outline are assembled the stakes of Modigliani's art.[1]

The same is true for a doctor examining a patient: everything begins with the skin and we are reminded that touch brings with it a responsibility for tenderness, and the more intimate the touch, the greater the necessity for care, kindness, and gentleness. Nowadays, I think of this whenever I see a Modigliani portrait.

Describing Dr Sassall in *A Fortunate Man*, John wrote: 'His hands are at home on a body.'[2]

---

[1] Berger, J. 'Modigliani's Alphabet of Love'. In: *The Sense of Sight*. Vintage International, 1985, p. 104.
[2] Berger, J., and Mohr, J. *A Fortunate Man*. 1967. Penguin Books, 1969, p. 18.

And it is true that years of practice (in both senses) brings an enormous familiarity with all sorts and conditions of bodies, their contours, their surfaces and what can be felt beneath the skin. The hands have acquired a craft skill, so much so, that when I retired from clinical practice, I missed that skill in my hands and found that I needed to seek out different manual skills in knitting and bread-making that left me feeling a little less bereft.

Later in the same book, he wrote:

> We give the doctor access to our bodies. Apart from the doctor, we only grant such access voluntarily to lovers—and many are frightened to do even this. Yet the doctor is a comparative stranger.[3]

My perception is that some doctors, including some of those who taught me at medical school in the 1970s, regard access to the body of a patient as a right and will embark on an examination without a hint of the required tenderness. For me, this is the complete reverse of the actual situation in which every patient has a right to the privacy of their own body. On each and every occasion the doctor should seek explicit consent to the invasive touch of a clinical examination and should look for any signs of distress or discomfort and should stop immediately if asked too.

John wrote[4] to me:

> I spent the New Year with my friend Simon McBurney who is the director of the Theatre de Complicité. You perhaps know of their work. Their last extraordinary work was Mnemonic.

---

[3] Berger, J., and Mohr, J. A Fortunate Man. 1967. Penguin Books, 1969, p. 64.
[4] 11 January 2001.

I replied:[5]

On Tuesday, we went to see Mnemonic[6] at the National Theatre and it was completely captivating. I copied out part of the text:

> And what does nakedness remind us of? It reminds us that our fears are natural, that we are vulnerable. . . . Naked, our needs are clear, our fears so natural. . . . seeing a naked body of another person, we make an inventory of our own. Shoulder blade, ribs, clavicle. We list the sensations we feel in each part, one by one, all of them indescribable, all of them familiar, all of them constituting a home.

Wonderful. Although I have a small bad feeling that doctors should know this but we don't—or didn't!

Knowing this, it is a helpful discipline to imaginatively identify a patient's nakedness with one's own because then it is easier to understand the required gentleness and respect.

Writing in his essay on 'Rembrandt and the Body' in the book *The Shape of the Pocket*, John imagined being in a hospital emergency department:

> Each one is living in her or his own corporeal space, in which the landmarks are a pain or a disability, an unfamiliar sensation or a numbness. . . . It is the space of each sentient body's awareness of itself. It is not boundless like subjective space: it is always finally bound by the laws of the body, but its landmarks, its emphasis, its inner proportions are continually changing. Pain sharpens our awareness of such space. It is the space of our first vulnerability and solitude. Also of disease. But it is also, potentially, the space of pleasure, well-being and the sensation of being loved. . . .

[5] 11 February 2001.
[6] Complicité. *Mnemonic*. Methuen Publishing, 2001.

It can be felt by touch more clearly than it can be seen by sight. He [Rembrandt] was the painterly master of this corporeal space.[7]

The range of sensations that an individual body can perceive seems infinite and the feelings that can be evoked by touch similarly so. As doctors, we can never know what is felt or evoked by our exploring touch, even if we ask, but we should still ask because each time we do, we will learn something new.

In the Kraków chapter of *Here Is Where We Meet*, John reported a friend's response to a copy of a drawing he had made of an Antonella da Messina painting.

The friend said:

Not a trace of pity on the angel's face or in his hands . . . only tenderness. You've caught the tenderness but not the gravity.[8]

I wrote[9] to John after he sent me a copy of the drawing:

Thank you so much for sending your Antonella drawing: 'Dead Christ supported by an Angel'. It sent me back to your Kraków story—tenderness with gravity but without pity. Tenderness without pity—suddenly it is very important and it is because the absence of pity seems to mean that the relationship is between equals—it's a relationship of solidarity—maybe touch can be about tenderness but never about pity. Thank you.

I was learning so much: touch must always be gentle and tender and intensely serious but should somehow avoid the slight condescension implicit in pity.

---

[7] Berger, J. 'Rembrandt and the Body'. In: Berger, J. *The Shape of the Pocket*. Bloomsbury, 2001, p. 107.
[8] Berger, J. Here Is Where We Meet. Bloomsbury Publishing, 2005, p. 81.
[9] 29 March 2006.

Figure 7 Copy by John Berger of *Dead Christ supported by an Angel* by
Antonello da Messina
Source: © John Berger and John Berger Estate.

11

THINKING

What does it mean to think? Plato described thinking as the dialogue of the soul with itself. It is totally interior to each individual and invisible to others. And yet it can be extraordinarily difficult and even painful. It is how we all attempt to make sense of the world and our place within it. It can be the source of our greatest discoveries but also our grossest errors.

Oddly it seems that now doctors are less and less required to think about the care and treatment each patient needs. With the rise of so-called evidence-based medicine and the proliferation of guidelines, medicine has become more and more mechanistic. It sometimes seems that doctors are even being actively encouraged not to think. Yet as I grow older, I know that when I am sick, I want a doctor who has a sound grasp of the evidence derived from biomedical science but is prepared to think about me as an individual and about my values, my aims, and the complexity of my context in terms of my home, my social setting, and my life history. We are constantly told that guidelines are only created to provide guidance to doctors and they are not in any sense rules. Yet this is not how doctors experience them: the degree of adherence to guidelines is increasingly regarded as a marker for the quality of practice, and young doctors seem increasingly fearful of deviating from guidelines for fear of complaints and litigation.

Someone said 'thinking government is an oxymoron' but I don't remember who. I heard it somewhere and thought, from where I'm sitting, that feels right. I worry that, within medicine, with the rise of these thousands of approved guidelines for the management of almost every conceivable condition, the idea of 'a thinking doctor' is also becoming an oxymoron. Within a worsening atmosphere of blaming and shaming, young doctors and not-so-young ones who should know better, are becoming afraid of deviating from guidelines in case something goes wrong. The fallacy of this argument is that guidelines are based on the generalizations of biomedical science and they cannot be made to accommodate the multitude of different individuals from different contexts and cultures, with different life stories, aspirations, and hopes. Again, I know that I do not want a doctor who is too afraid to do anything other than slavishly follow guidelines, I want a doctor who will think.

At the same time, the sociologist Zygmunt Bauman argued:

> To be responsible does not mean to follow the rules; it may often require us to disregard the rules or to act in a way the rules do not warrant. Only such responsibility makes the citizen into that basis on which can be built a human community resourceful and thoughtful enough to cope with the present challenges.[1]

He seemed to be urging doctors to disregard the broad and banal guideline which does not quite fit this particular patient.

---

[1] Bauman, Z. *Alone Again: Ethics after Uncertainty*. Demos, 1994, p. 45.

And this resonates deeply with my experience of medical practice over almost thirty-five years.

In his novel *G*, John seemed to touch on my fear:

> Whatever I perceive or imagine amazes me by its particularity. …
> I do not wish to become a prisoner of the nominal, believing that
> things are what I name them.

In his essay 'Revolutionary Undoing' in *The Look of Things*, John introduced the work of the German-American art historian Max Raphael. Quoting from his posthumously published *The Demands of Art*,[2] John records:

> The characteristics of the individual idea are:
>
> 1. It is simultaneously an idea and a feeling.
> 2. It contains the contrasts between the particular and the general, the individual and the universal, the original and the banal.
> 3. It is a progression toward ever deeper meanings.
> 4. It is the nodal point from which secondary ideas and feelings develop.

Both Raphael and John were referring to the individual idea that underpins a work of art, but, for me, the list evokes a definition of a medical diagnosis to which I aspire: a useful signpost but, at the same time, loose, mutable, transitory, and flexible. Such a definition would be much more subtle than the concrete labels of current usage, incorporating not only ideas from biomedical science, while still leaving space for scientific progress and new ideas, but also the subjective feelings of patient and doctor. Diagnosis always pits the particular against the generalities of science, the individual against the universal and would be much improved

---

[2] Raphael, M. *The Demands of Art*, trans. N. Guterman, Routledge & Kegan Paul, 1968.

if we also thought about the contrast between the original and the banal. I think that, if the process of diagnosis incorporated the latter, much more attention would be paid to the detail of the patient's individual predicament and there would be hope of progression to deeper meanings, secondary ideas and feelings, and even scientific insight. These would be diagnoses that encourage further thinking alongside biomedical progress, rather than, as now, shutting off further thought once a diagnosis has been made and the correct guideline selected.

If I now return to G., I read, (and for once, the personal pronoun is right), and I immediately recognize:

> She trusted certain feelings in herself precisely because they did not lead to conclusions.[3]

How do we assess the trustworthiness of our feelings? This seems to be touching on the importance of emotions in calibrating and restraining rationality, and of valuing uncertainty for the space and freedom it gives within which to avoid unwarranted conclusions. It encapsulates my conviction that premature diagnosis causes a great deal of harm, particularly in primary care. Symptoms suggestive of disease are very common and, almost certainly, more are caused by the stresses and strains of life than by an actual disease process. Who has not developed a headache just because they are worrying about something? If symptoms precipitated by the difficulties of life are wrongly interpreted as disease, there will be all sorts of consequences, most of them harmful. Unless the situation is clearly urgent and serious, there is much to be said for delaying conclusions and waiting to see

---

[3] Berger, J. G. Bloomsbury Publishing, 1996, p. 97.

if time will work its magic as a diagnostic and therapeutic tool. A firm diagnosis should only be made if it is going to lead to a course of action of clear benefit to the patient.[4]

In 'A Story for Aesop' in *Keeping a Rendezvous*, John contemplated the Velazquez portrait with the same title and, using the acute empathic imagination that was his genius, he described the life and thoughts of the legendary storyteller:

> Everything he has seen contributes to his sense of the enigma of life: for this enigma he finds partial answers—each story he tells is one—yet each answer, each story, uncovers another question, and so he is continually failing and this failure maintains his curiosity.
>
> ...
>
> The story becomes a story because we are not quite sure; because we remain sceptical either way. Life's experience of itself (and what else are stories if not that?) is always sceptical.[5]

All the time, unbeknownst to himself, John was describing, very precisely, what was happening to me when I sat in a consulting room, or next to the bed in a patient's home while I groped towards an understanding of what was happening. And, for many patients, a story, within which they are recognized and can recognize themselves, as victim or hero, is more useful than a medical diagnosis. As John completely understood creating a story is a mode of thinking which allows for different and equally valid outcomes and which resists facile conclusions.

In *Hold Everything Dear*, John described the film-maker Pier Paolo Pasolini:

[4] Rudebeck, C. E. 'General Practice and the Dialogue of Clinical Practice: On Symptoms, Symptom Presentations and Bodily Empathy'. *Scandinavian Journal of Primary Health Care.* Suppl 1, 1992, 1–87.
[5] Berger, J. 'A Story for Aesop'. In: Keeping a Rendezvous. 1985. Vintage International, 1992, p. 59.

[He] looks at the world with unflinching lucidity. (There are angels drawn by Rembrandt who have the same gaze.) And he does so because reality is all we have to love. There is nothing else.[6]

There is no contradiction whatever between the mutability of story and this commitment to unflinching lucidity. In an essay[7] that I sent to John very early in our correspondence, I took my title from the closing stanza of a poem by the Polish poet Zbigniev Herbert, 'Mr Cogito and the Imagination':

> he would like to remain faithful
> to uncertain clarity[8]

The aspiration should be not only to see, but also to think, clearly and truthfully, while at the same time treasuring uncertainty.

I think John's mother would approve. In *Here Is Where We Meet*, John wrote about meeting the ghost of his dead mother in Lisbon. She said:

> All you have to know is whether you're lying or whether you're trying to tell the truth, you can't afford to make a mistake about that distinction any longer.[9]

For me, it is crucial that the contrast is between lying and *trying* to tell the truth, even if not necessarily achieving the latter.

[6] Berger, J. *Hold Everything Dear: Dispatches on Survival and Resistance*. Verso, 2007, p. 79.

[7] Heath, I. 'Uncertain Clarity': Contradiction, Meaning, and Hope'. *British Journal of General Practice*, 1999, 49: 651–657.

[8] Herbert, Z. 'Mr Cogito and the Imagination'. In: Report from the Besieged City and Other Poems, trans. J. Carpenter and B. Carpenter, Oxford University Press, 1987, p. 17.

[9] Berger, J. Here Is Where We Meet. Bloomsbury Publishing, 2005, p. 42.

In October 2002, John sent me a text which was later published in *Le Monde Diplomatique* with the title 'The Pain of Living in the Present World.'[10] Responding two weeks later, I wrote:[11]

> When you write: 'It happens that in their lives, people suffer from wrongs which are classified in separate categories, and suffer them simultaneously and inseparably', you describe exactly the people who come to see me. Today, doctors are assessed according to how they treat hypertension or diabetes or asthma. Those doing the assessing seem not to notice that many people have all three—inseparably—and that they are also grieving or lonely or frightened—and that all of this is a single condition, not many. No one aspect can be treated, let alone healed, in isolation from the others.

The insoluble problem for clinical medicine is that all the evidence on which guidelines are based is derived from the study of populations and can tell us nothing about what will happen to, or what is appropriate for, a single individual patient. The application of generalized knowledge to particular people cannot be achieved by following rules: it will always require wisdom and judgement. And as T. S. Eliot so famously recognized,[12] we are swamped with information, we have some knowledge but we are always lacking wisdom. The sad truth is that since the time of Aristotle, almost two and a half thousand years ago, we have made enormous strides in knowledge but vanishingly little progress in relation to the wisdom necessary for judgement. Knowledge without wisdom is dangerous. As the philosopher Stephen Toulmin put it:

[10] https://mondediplo.com/2003/02/15pain
[11] 7 November 2002.
[12] Eliot, T. S. The Rock: A Pageant Play. Faber & Faber, 1934.

None of this would be news to Aristotle, who knew the differences between intellectual grasp of a theory (or episteme), mastery of arts and techniques (techne), and the wisdom needed to put techniques to work in concrete cases dealing with actual problems.[13]

Sadly, today, we seem to have much less awareness of these crucial differences and continually expect that our intellectual grasp of theory will help us to deal with actual problems but this is so rarely true. American philosopher Martha Nussbaum maintained that:

> Indeed, part of the 'art' of Aristotelian practical wisdom ... seems to consist in being keenly responsive to the limits of one's 'material' and figuring out what is best given the possibilities, rather than rigidly aiming at some inflexible set of norms.[14]

And I find myself wondering where this leaves the usefulness of clinical guidelines? I suspect that Aristotle would not have been an enthusiast. Nussbaum also argued that

> each of the strategies used to make practical wisdom more scientific and more in control ... leads to a distinct impoverishment of the world of practice.[15]

[13] Toulmin, S. *Cosmopolis: The Hidden Agenda of Modernity*. The University of Chicago Press, 1990, p. 190.
[14] Nussbaum, M. C. *Poetic Justice: The Literary Imagination and Public Life*. Beacon Press, 1995, p. 333.
[15] Nussbaum, M. C. *Poetic Justice: The Literary Imagination and Public Life*. Beacon Press, 1995, p. 310.

12

WORDS

In *Lilac and Flag*, the third part of his *Into their Labours* trilogy of novels, John wrote:

> Men and women are not like this dog because they have words. With their words they change everything, and nothing. Whatever the circumstances, words add and take away. Either spoken words or ones heard in the head. They are always incongruous, because they never fit. This is why words cause pain and why they offer salvation.[1]

Words never quite fit because they were, and continue to be, created for communication and dialogue. They seek to find common ground and so build understanding between two different individuals and may end up representing neither perfectly. The Russian philosopher, Mikhail Bakhtin described[2] the ways in which words oscillate continually between centripetal and centrifugal forces. As each one of us uses a word to try to convey our own personal truth, we select appropriates words for our own purposes, we generate a centrifugal force which continually develops and fragments language; yet, at the same time, all

---

[1] Berger, J. *Lilac and Flag*. 1992. Vintage International, 1999, p. 147.
[2] Bakhtin, M. M. *The Dialogic Imagination: Four Essays*. Austin: University of Texas Press, 1981.

language is social and built on the attempt to achieve shared and therefore centripetal understanding.

It does not take long for a young doctor to discover this dangerous slipperiness of words and the need for constant vigilance when choosing them. I am reminded that I once attended an academic seminar on the then relatively new discipline of medical humanities. The seminar was intended to bring together humanities scholars with doctors, some of whom were young and others who had considerable experience. The contributions from the academics were interesting and challenging but most of them were delivered in abstruse and inaccessible language. I raised this as an issue and was told, perhaps a little condescendingly, that some topics can only be addressed in a specialist language and suddenly, I was very aware of the young doctors in the room, all of whom were in the process of learning the absolute necessity of being able to explain their sophisticated biomedical understanding of the patients' illnesses in language that was understandable to each particular patient in turn. They already knew that if they got the words wrong, they could cause pain, and that if they chose better, both patient and doctors would begin to have a better chance of understanding what was happening and a much better prospect of finding a way through.

Careful listening to patients' stories, or indeed anyone's stories can help us to keep doing the necessary thinking because stories so often have to do with the gaps where new knowledge is to be found, both biomedical and biographical. Stories begin in the gap between a word and its object because any experience is larger than the account of it that anyone can give in words; the same gap between a word and its object, which has been explored by philosophers and in linguistics for centuries. And this foundational gap leads us on to explore the gap between what is and what might have been, between different truths and different meanings, and they are a constantly available antidote to the all-too-prevalent false certainties of contemporary medicine.

In *The Shape of the Pocket*, John quoted Subcomandante Marcos:

> 'Were these words the best ones to say what we wanted to say?' 'Were they the right words at this time?' 'Were they understandable?'[3]

These were the questions the Zapatistas asked themselves whenever they sent a communiqué to the outside world—but, remarkably, they are also the exact words that doctors, young or old, should be asking themselves at the end of each consultation.

In one of my early letters[4] to John, I worried:

> I am more and more convinced that the diagnostic labels used by psychiatry are almost completely useless.

John replied:[5]

> Maybe labels are useful early in the morning of a work—when the pile to be shifted seems as high as a little mountain—but by noon the labels should have been discarded.

This was precious. I replied:[6]

> What you say about labels is very helpful—it tells me that young doctors need labels and that I must allow them to use them but it

[3] Berger, J. 'Correspondence with Subcomandante Marcos'. In: Berger, J. *The Shape of the Pocket*. Bloomsbury, 2001, p. 258.
[4] 26 March 2000.
[5] 5 April 2000.
[6] 23 April 2000.

also tells me that I am right to feel more and more impatient with them as I get older—but what do I put in their place? How can I pin down and communicate my understanding without them? How does a word become degraded into a label?

In *Once in Europa*, in the story he called 'The Time of the Cosmonauts', John gave me my answer:

> If every event which occurred could be given a name, there would be no need for stories. As things are here, life outstrips our vocabulary. A word is missing and so the story has to be told.[7]

I wrote[8] to John about this:

> I know there is truth in this but I am struggling with the process of how the story makes up for the missing word—is it simply because the story can convey complexity and subtlety in a way that a single word can never match? Or is it because we only understand any single word because of the stories which surround it—'love' being the perfect example. Two weeks ago, I went to Buenos Aires for five days which was a crazy thing to do and I compounded it by reading Borges so the whole experience became intensely disorientating and dream-like—but the point is that in one of his stories, Borges seems to suggest that nouns are about space and verbs about time and so a single word will never do.
>
> But in medicine we try to make do with single words—albeit long words—most of the time. And yesterday I was reading a wonderful article by a Finnish GP colleague about a short story by Chekhov which contains the passage:
>
> > The patient gives her opinion of the problem by using a medical term 'palpitations', as if this simple diagnosis would completely decipher her malady. But we also learn that the

[7] Berger, J. *Once in Europa*. Vintage International, 1992, p. 64.
[8] 22 June 2000.

problem is not only palpitations but also terror. She 'nearly died of fright'.[9]

Grafting on Borges—I arrive at the conclusion that medical diagnoses are only about space and not about time—which is interesting—particularly as we always try to link diagnosis to prognosis in a dangerously fatalistic way.

Am I at all close to understanding what you meant?

John replied:[10]

Borges, as so often, is right. Nouns extend in space. Verbs in time. Pronouns, perhaps in eternity?

The last question took me by surprise which was almost certainly John's intention; to encourage me to take Borges' ideas a little further. I took it to mean that he was wondering about the existence of eternity within relationships and so in the use of pronouns. And, of course, I should have asked him, but I never did.

Life outstrips the medical vocabulary of diagnostic labels, which become increasingly dangerous to the extent that the story has not been told. If the label, once given, stops the original doctor, or the next one the patient sees, from listening to the story, great harm can be done; not just in the failure of recognition but because the label might be wrong or only a very small part of the problem. This is one of the reasons why the replacement of the traditional referral letter, from the general practitioner to the specialist, by a standardized referral form, represents such a degradation of care.

---

[9] Puustinen, R. 'Voices to Be Heard—The Many Positions of a Physician in Anton Chekhov's Short Story, "A Case History"'. *Journal of Medical Ethics: Medical Humanities*. 2000, 26: 37–42.
[10] July 2000.

Much medical discourse, constrained by computers, has become what John described as:

A language that can no longer explain what matters.[11]

And, perhaps demonstrating the truth of this, John wrote:[12]

The category Depression has become a trash lorry.

On another occasion, aware of the extent to which a diagnosis, like too many other medical labels, is little more than a not-so-subtle form of victim-blaming, I responded:[13]

Yes—depressed is a horrible, mean little word which seems to undermine yet further the dignity of all who suffer it. The only faintly useful thing about it is its passivity—the suggestion that an outside force has caused the depression which perhaps acknowl-edges a little that depression is so often caused by the injustices of society—but it is insufficient compensation.

In *Keeping a Rendezvous*, John summarized the problem of any spe-cialist language:

Any language as taught always has a tendency to close, to lose its original signifying power. When this happens, it can go straight to the cultivated mind, but it bypasses the thereness of things and events.[14]

---

[11] https://www.theguardian.com/theobserver/2003/apr/06/featuresreview.review1
[12] 11 January 2001.
[13] 7 January 2002.
[14] Berger, J. 'A Professional Secret'. In: *Keeping a Rendezvous*. 1985. Vintage International, 1993, p. 129.

To listen to John in any context was to see him thinking and searching for words and demonstrating how much work there is in putting words together and that it demands effort if it is to be done well. As a doctor talking to a patient, I need to understand the degree of effort involved as I choose my words and be prepared to make it.

Putting words together well is almost a definition of poetry and perhaps this is why John and I exchanged so many poems in our letters. In *And Our Faces*, John wrote:

> Poems, regardless of any outcome, cross the battlefields, tending the wounded, listening to the wild monologues of the triumphant or the fearful. They bring a kind of peace. Not by anaesthesia or easy reassurance, but by recognition and the promise that what has been experienced cannot disappear as if it had never been. Yet the promise is not of a monument. The promise is that language has acknowledged, has given shelter, to the experience which demanded, which cried out.[15]

Doctors, if they do nothing else, try to tend the wounded and in doing so, they need to use language that acknowledges the experience of being wounded, in whatever sense the wounding has occurred. Doctors need the example of poets.

In the same book, John argued:

> To break the silence of events, to speak of experience however bitter or lacerating, to put into words, is to discover the hope that these words may be heard, and that when heard, the events will be judged.[16]

[15] Berger, J. *And Our Faces, My Heart, Brief as Photos.* 1984. Vintage International, 1991, p. 21.
[16] Berger, J. *And Our Faces, My Heart, Brief as Photos.* 1984. Vintage International, 1991, p. 98.

So, when stories are told, the words must be heard and when it is a patient who recounts their bitter experience, it is the doctor who must hear and judge the trauma of the event not, as seems to happen too often, the person of the patient.

And again, in *And Our Faces*, I find:

> Poetry's impulse to use metaphor, to discover resemblance, is not to make comparisons (all comparisons as such are hierarchical) or to diminish the particularity of any event; it is to discover those correspondences of which the sum total would be proof of the indivisible totality of existence.[17]

And I think this is what happens over the working lifetime of a general practitioner who remains in one place, like the Fortunate Man in the deep countryside of the Forest of Dean, or even myself in the urban chaos of Kentish Town in London. We discover resemblances and correspondences and these become an indivisible totality of our experience: of everything we have seen and heard and learnt, the sum of which feels almost like the poem of our lives.

In *Keeping a Rendezvous*, John gave me yet another clue:

> The credibility of words involves a strange dialectic. It is the writer's openness to the ambiguity and uncertainty of any experience (even the experience of determination and certainty) which gives clarity, and thus a kind of certainty to his writing.[18]

---

[17] Berger, J. *And Our Faces, My Heart, Brief as Photos.* 1984. Vintage International, 1991, p. 96.
[18] Berger, J. 'Lost off Cape Wrath'. In: *Keeping a Rendezvous*, 1991. Vintage International 1992, p. 216.

And again, the same magic is working and he is speaking to me about being a doctor: about the need to be open to all the ambiguity and uncertainty of each patient's story and so achieve a kind of clarity of understanding from within that.

13

TIME

I wrote[1] to John:

> Whenever I read your writing—even if I feel that I don't quite follow your full meaning—you make me think and that is a great gift from you to me. Thank you!

The notion of Time provides an example of my struggle to grasp this full meaning.

The timetable of my career in general practice was relentless and for the whole of my almost thirty-five years, appointments were booked at ten-minute intervals with longer breaks for recovery alongside morning coffee, lunch, and afternoon tea. Ten minutes passes quickly and even more so when the doctor is inexperienced and not very confident. Early on, I was taught that if I overran the time slot, I would need to be able to justify (to myself, at least) the extra time given to one patient in terms of the time taken away from another. Time passes even more quickly now that it is also taken away from the patient to feed 'the beast' which is the computer now present in every consulting room. The early days of the computerization of general practice, in the late 1970s and early 1980s, felt exciting and innovative and a few of the bureaucratic aspects of practice became less onerous but very soon computers

---

[1] 8 February 2004.

began to enable detailed surveillance by those in power, rapidly followed by the mandating of activities by policymakers which all too often proved futile and inappropriate, and had nothing to do with the predicament of the patient and their hopes for the consultation. I have never felt able to justify the activities of feeding the beast in terms of the time for the patient that is lost forever. So, time in general practice is a beleaguered and highly conflicted commodity.

Fortunately, time has depth as well as duration. In *A Fortunate Man*, John proposed:

> The objective co-ordinates of time and space, which are necessary to fix a presence, are relatively stable. But the subjective experience of time is liable to be so grossly distorted—above all by suffering—that it becomes, both to the sufferer and to any person partially identifying himself with the sufferer, extremely difficult to correlate with time proper.[2]

An understanding of the undoubted truth of this helps in the process of allocating precious time equitably. Suffering and pain often slow time inexorably because of the amount of space within time that the distress occupies. Consequently, the patient needs more time with the doctor, because the interaction has somehow to be fitted around the space occupied by the suffering or the pain.

In *About Looking*, in his essay about a single painting by the Turkish artist Seker Ahmet Pasa (1841–1907), John wrote:

> For Heidegger the present, the now, is not a measurable unit of time, but the result of presence, of the existent actively presenting itself.[3]

[2] Berger, J., and Mohr, J. *A Fortunate Man*. 1967. Penguin Books, 1969, p. 131.
[3] Berger, J. *About Looking*. 1980. Bloomsbury Publishing, 2009, p. 93.

And somehow this helps me to clarify some of my perplexity about time. When suffering is exerting a huge presence in the life of a patient, it is also a huge presence within the consultation; a presence that almost swallows up time.

In *The Look of Things*, John recruited Walter Benjamin to the discussion of time:

> The immorality of the conviction that ends justify means lies in the arrogance of the assumption that time is always on one's own side and that, therefore, the present moment—the time of the Now, as Benjamin called it, can be compromised or forgotten or denied.[4]

This helps me to understand my own distress about the role of computers in consulting rooms driven by the arrogant assumption that time is always on the side of power and that the patient's time of the Now can be compromised and denied without any consequences.

In *And Our Faces*, John took his thinking about time a step further:

> Man is unique insofar as he constitutes two events. The event of his biological organism—and the event of his consciousness. Thus in man two times coexist, corresponding with these two events. The time during which he is conceived, grows, matures, ages, dies. And the time of his consciousness.
>
> The first time understands itself. Which is why animals have no philosophical problems. The second time has been understood in different ways in different periods. It is indeed the first task of any culture to propose an understanding of the time of consciousness, of the relations of past to future realised as such.[5]

---

[4] Berger, J. *Selected Essays and Articles: The Look of Things*. Penguin Books, 1972, p. 92.
[5] Berger, J. *And Our Faces, My Heart, Brief as Photos*. 1984. Vintage International, 1991, p. 9.

And he goes on to describe poetry as an important part of the culture that helps us to understand the time of consciousness:

> The poet places language beyond the reach of time: or, more accurately, the poet approaches language as if it were a place, an assembly point, where time has no finality, where time itself is encompassed and contained.
>
> If poetry sometimes speaks of its own immortality, the claim is more far-reaching than that of the genius of a particular poet in a particular cultural history. Immortality here should be distinguished from posthumous fame. Poetry can speak of immortality because it abandons itself to language in the belief that language embraces all experiences, past, present and future.
>
> To speak of the promise of poetry would be misleading, for a promise projects into the future, and it is precisely the coexistence of future, present and past that poetry proposes. A promise that applies to the present and past as well as to the future can better be called an assurance.[6]

Is this why I have found poetry so helpful in bridging those time zones within the consultation without losing confidence in the uncertain territory beneath my feet?

I wrote[7] to John that I had been speaking at a conference on Complexity Theory and Primary Health Care:

> An increasing number of health professionals are looking to complexity theory to provide some sort of defence against the intense reductiveness of traditional biomedical science. Somehow, complexity seems to provide some very helpful new metaphors for looking at old and intractable situations in a new way.

---

[6] Berger, J. *And Our Faces, My Heart, Brief as Photos.* 1984. Vintage International, 1991, pp. 22–23.
[7] 26 September 2002.

I talked about how complexity theory acknowledges the power of time much more than traditional Newtonian science. Everything is evolving and has a unique history and we can never extrapolate either backwards or forwards in time with any degree of certainty and time flows only one way. And all this means that every interaction between people—including between doctor and patient—contains the possibility of regret and lost opportunity. Information or pharmaceuticals or fear—once given—cannot be taken back—which somehow seems to mean that we should be less certain—less arrogant—in what we do.

And then I copied out an English translation of Fernando Pessoa's wonderful poem 'In the Terrible Night' because it seemed to me to be saying much the same things as complexity theory.

14

SPACE AND PLACE

In *The Look of Things*, John argued:

> Space is part of the continuity of the events within it. It is in itself
> an event comparable to other events. It is not a mere container.[1]

And it is perhaps not surprising that someone who described
himself as a storyteller but spent a huge amount of time trying
to find meaning in the appearance of space and place within
paintings and other art, should turn out to be someone prepared
to pay equal attention to both history and geography.

The political geographer Edward Soja, writing of the ascen-
dancy of history over space and place since the nineteenth
century,[2] described John, alongside Michel Foucault, as having
produced 'assertive postmodern geographies [that] have been
largely hidden from view by their more comforting and familiar
identification as historians'. Soja noted the revealing structure of
John's *And Our Faces, My Heart, Brief as Photos* with Part One being
about Time and Part Two about Space, and with the parts being
titled Once and Here respectively. And in *The Look of Things*, Soja
found what is almost a manifesto:

---

[1] Berger, J. *Selected Essays and Articles: The Look of Things*. Penguin Books, 1972, p. 153.
[2] Soja, E. W. *Postmodern Geographies: The Reassertion of Space in Critical Social Theory*. Verso,
1994.

It is scarcely any longer possible to tell a straight story sequentially unfolding in time. And this is because—we are too aware of what is continually traversing the storyline laterally. That is to say, instead of being aware of a point as an infinitely small part of a straight line, we are aware of it as an infinitely small part of an infinite number of lines, as the centre of a star of lines. Such awareness is the result of our constantly having to take into account the simultaneity and extension of events and possibilities.

There are so many reasons why this should be so: the range of modern means of communication: the scale of modern power: the degree of personal political responsibility that must be accepted for events all over the world: the fact that the world has become indivisible: the unevenness of economic development within that world: the scale of the exploitation. All these play a part. Prophesy now involves a geographical rather than historical projection; it is space not time that hides consequences from us.[3]

This reminds me of the *Mapping Journey Project* of the French-Moroccan artist Bouchra Khalili[4] in which she first made video recordings of a number of refugees describing their huge and punitive journeys in search of safety and she then plotted those journeys as points on a dark blue background creating what becomes a constellation, which, as we have already seen is an important metaphor for John.

In *A Fortunate Man*, John very definitely situated his story of the general practitioner within a landscape and Jean Mohr's photos followed him as he moved between and within his patients' homes criss-crossing the community that he shares with them. More than forty years have passed and today general practitioners do many fewer home visits and often live outside their practice areas. What have we lost? How much does it matter?

[3] Berger, J. *Selected Essays and Articles: The Look of Things*. Penguin Books, 1972, p. 40.
[4] http://www.bouchrakhalili.com/the-constellations/

Yet, every general practitioner who has done regular home visits knows that more can be discovered on a single home visit than from a succession of consultations in the surgery. Circumstances, memories, and aspirations are all inscribed on a home and tell stories of cohesiveness, displacement, or separation. For each patient, the doctor begins to learn about what or who is near or far and about how much pain or pleasure is contained within these distances. That tea towel map of New Zealand pinned to the wall of a kitchen in Kentish Town provides just one tiny example. Yi-Fu Tuan [known as the father of humanistic geography] has written about the difference between place and space: the former providing the fixity necessary for security and the latter the opportunity for movement and exploration.[5] From the safety and stability of a known place, each of us is aware of the openness, freedom, and threat of space, and vice versa. Each patient seeks their own balance: some cling to the security, however limited, of the known; others take great risks to find new freedom and opportunity in the unknown and begin the tough process of changing strange space into safe place. More people than ever before are moving great distances and across national boundaries, often for pleasure, but too often forced by intimidation, persecution, war, or poverty. This unprecedented level of human movement disconnects people from home and family, fractures the cohesion of community structures and comes with both rewards and costs. As general practitioners, we see both the losers and the beneficiaries.

The perception of both place and space is affected by illness and disability often with a heightened sense of the security of

[5] Tuan, Y.-F. *Space and Place: The Perspective of Experience*. University of Minnesota Press, 2001.

place and the threat of space.[6] Each patient's interaction with the health service is played out through geography. Distance from the surgery or the hospital may be a powerful disincentive to attending, particularly for those who are feeling vulnerable, and especially if they are also dependent on public transport. Where geography intersects with biography a whole family may be left with an enduring fear of a particular hospital which will undermine their ability to use available health services. General practitioners' referral patterns already reflect this detailed understanding of the individual geography of patients.[7] By deliberately acknowledging the fact that all life stories also have a geography and by seeking out those geographies, as John did in so many of his essays, we are taken deeper into the detail of the lives of individuals, families, and communities, witnessing the intertwining of time and space. A person known in this way can never again be viewed as a unit of this or that diagnosis.

Later, in *The Look of Things*, John described Walter Benjamin as also bridging history and geography and so reasserting the importance of space and place:

> His attitude to works of art was never a mechanically social-historical one. He never tried to seek simple causal relations between the social forces of a period and a given work. He did not want to explain the appearance of the work; he wanted to discover the place that its existence needed to occupy in our knowledge.[8]

And this is what the general practitioner needs to do; to look beyond the short time-bound causal chains that abound

---

[6] Toombs, S. K. *The Meaning of Illness: A Phenomenological Account of the Different Perspectives of Physician and Patient*. Dordrecht: Kluwer Academic Publishers, 1993.
[7] Chishty, V., and Packer, C. 'Age, Distance from a Hospital, and Level of Deprivation are Influential Factors'. *BMJ*. 1995, 310: 867.
[8] Berger, J. *Selected Essays and Articles: The Look of Things*. Penguin Books, 1972, p. 91.

in medicine and situate the patient within both the norms of biology and the history and geography of an individual life.

In his 1969 book *Art and Revolution* John wrote about the nature of sculpture:

> Its frontiers with that space are definitive. Its only function is to use space in such a way that it confers meaning upon it. It does not move or become relative. In every way possible it emphasises its own finiteness. And by so doing it invokes the notion of infinity and challenges it.
>
> We, perceiving this total opposition between the sculpture and the surrounding space, translate its promise into terms of time. It will stand against time as it stands against space.[9]

Writing about Auguste Rodin in *The Guardian Review* in September 2006, Geoff Dyer included this quotation from John and continued:

> Rodin, according to Rilke, saw better than anybody that the beauty of men, animals and things was 'endangered by time and circumstances'. Seeking to preserve this threatened beauty, he adapted his things to the less imperilled, quieter and more eternal world of 'space'.[10]

Rodin seems to feel that space may be gentler than time. But perhaps that is just for sculpture and not for those people who spent whole lives being goaded from one place to another. The refugees I tried to care for in Kentish Town were among the most traumatized I have ever listened to.

[9] Berger, J. *Art and Revolution*. Pelican Books, 1969, p. 74.
[10] Dyer, G. 'Auguste Rodin: Souls of Stone'. The Guardian Review, 16 September 2006.

In *Hold Everything Dear,* John wrote and asked:

> From the human capacity to arrange, to place, come language and communication. The word *place* is both verb and noun. The capacity of arrangement and the capacity to recognize and name a site. Aren't both inseparable in their origin from the human need to respect and defend their dead?[11]

And this fundamental importance of place reinforces the terrible price of displacement and its capacity to disorient lives and relationships, sometimes to breaking point.

---

[11] Berger, J. *Hold Everything Dear: Dispatches on Survival and Resistance.* Verso, 2007, p. 76.

15

HOPE

In *A Fortunate Man*, John described

the extraordinarily complex convergence of philosophical tradi-
tions, feelings, half-realized ideas, atavistic instincts, imaginative
intimations, which lie behind the simplest hope or disappointment
of the simplest person.[1]

And Alastair MacIntyre, writing within a philosophical tradition
in his *Seven Traits for Designing our Descendants*, which was published
as a Hastings Center Report in 1979, wrote that hope exists

precisely in the face of evil which tempts us to despair. The presupposition of hope identifies a belief in a reality that transcends
evidence.[2]

Somehow, for me, this captured the enduring courage of John's
commitment to hope. He stared evil in the face with an exact
understanding of the degree to which so many lives are blighted
by the greed, exploitation, coercion, ignorance, and the prejudice
of others. He had an immediate and instinctive identification with
those trapped on the losing side. He was undoubtedly tempted

[1] Berger, J., and Mohr, J. *A Fortunate Man*. 1967. Penguin Books, 1969, p. 110.
[2] MacIntyre, A. 'Designing our Descendants: Seven Traits for the Future'. *Hastings Center
Report*. 1979, 9(1): 5–7.

to despair but yet he seemed to find in the stories of those who survive and endure a constant wellspring of hope.

He was acutely aware of the freedom that hope can confer on even the most constrained of lives and the way hope is fostered by the smallest pleasures—a touch, a flower, a ray of sunshine:

> Art does not imitate nature, it imitates a creation, sometimes to propose an alternative world, sometimes simply to amplify, to confirm, to make social the brief hope offered by nature.[3]

Yet he knew that hope is never far from despair. In *Once in Europa*, he wrote:

> Hell begins with hope. If we didn't have any hopes we wouldn't suffer.[4]

In *The Look of Things*, he declared:

> The world is not intolerable until the possibility of transforming it exists but is denied.[5]

And in *And Our Faces*, he went further:

> They know that there has never been a winter in Anatolia without snow, a summer without animals dying of drought, a workers' movement without repression. Utopias exist only in carpets. But they know too that what they have been subjected to in their lives is intolerable. And the naming of the intolerable is itself the hope.

[3] Berger, J. 'The White Bird'. In: *The Sense of Sight.* 1985. Vintage International, 1993, p. 9.
[4] Berger, J. *Once in Europa.* Vintage International, 1992, p. 144.
[5] Berger, J. *Selected Essays and Articles: The Look of Things.* Penguin Books, 1972, p. 52.

JOHN BERGER

When something is termed intolerable, actions must follow. These actions are subject to all the vicissitudes of life. But the pure hope resides first and mysteriously in the capacity to name the intolerable as such: and this capacity comes from afar—from the past and from the future. This is why politics and courage are inevitable. The time of the torturers is agonizingly but exclusively the present.[6]

There is something here in John's exploration of the nature of hope which reminds me of something that George Steiner wrote in *Grammars of Creation*:

There is an actual sense in which every human use of the future tense of the verb 'to be' is a negation, however limited, of mortality. Even as every use of an 'if'-sentence tells of a refusal of the brute inevitability, of the despotism of the fact. 'Shall', 'will' and 'if', circling in intricate fields of semantic force around a hidden centre or nucleus of potentiality, are the passwords to hope.[7]

And, throughout a long career, John set out to use words as just these passwords to hope.

Early in *A Fortunate Man*, he compared the role of a doctor to that of the master mariners in the novels of Joseph Conrad, writing:

Or consider Conrad's description of one of the worst moments in 'Typhoon'. With the exception of the one word 'gale', it might describe the crisis of an illness, with the voice of Captain MacWhirr transformed into that of a doctor:

And again he heard that voice, forced and ringing feebly, but with a penetrating effect of quietness in the enormous discord of noises, as if sent out from some remote spot of peace beyond the black wastes of the gale; again he heard

[6] Berger, J. *And Our Faces, My Heart, Brief as Photos*. 1984. Vintage International, 1991, p. 18.
[7] Steiner, G. *Grammars of Creation: Originating in the Gifford Lectures of 1990*. Faber & Faber, 2001, p. 7.

a man's voice - the frail and indomitable sound that can be made to carry an infinity of thought, resolution and purpose, that shall be pronouncing confident words on the last day when heavens fall, and justice is done - again he heard it, and it was crying to him, as if from very, very far—'All right'.[8]

This is the doctor compared to the captain and this role as hero seems to have been Dr Sassall's aspiration at the start of his career. Gradually, this was moderated by his experience of the chronicity and intransigence of so many of the more apparently mundane problems he faced, yet the power of the hero to generate hope in those who lack it remains very important. The doctor speaks from a position of greater biological knowledge alongside experience of a huge variety of illnesses and, because of this, however terrifying the situation, when the doctor declares a situation to be 'All right', there is clearly at least a prospect of hope.

The opposite of hope is despair. In an article published in *Race & Class*, in 2006,[9] John wrote:

A hope against hope (which is still far from a promise) collapses or is collapsed; despair fills the space in the soul which was occupied by that hope. Despair has nothing to do with nihilism.

Then in *King: A Street Story*, his 1999 novel about homelessness narrated by an extremely wise dog, he created this devastating formula to represent the accumulation of despair:

The first hopelessness is damp.
Damp + cold = despair.
Despair + hunger = no god ever.
No god ever + alcohol = self-kill.[10]

---

[8] Berger, J., and Mohr, J. *A Fortunate Man*. 1967. Penguin Books, 1969, pp. 53–54.
[9] Berger, J. 'Dispatches'. Race & Class. 2006, 48(1): 31.
[10] Berger, J. *King: A Street Story*. 1999. Vintage International, 2000, p. 32.

Every homeless person's sleeping bag that I see on the London streets seems to testify to the validity of the formula and to the appalling health consequences of homelessness.

John had sent me the text of his essay 'A Master of Pitilessness?' which was later published in *Hold Everything Dear*.[11] I wrote[12] to John:

> And your paper about Francis Bacon has also helped my thinking—somehow your writing always does! I used to hate Francis Bacon paintings—I couldn't really bear to look at them—they seemed gratuitously cruel. But almost ten years ago, I went to a conference in Oslo and, in that wonderful Scandinavian way, a conference about learning in medicine started with a guided tour of an exhibition of the London School at the Astrup-Fearnley Museum. In a snobbish way, I hate guided tours too but this felt obligatory and, of course, I learnt a lot and, in particular, I was obliged to stand and look at some Bacon paintings for much longer than I had ever done before. And I realised that I recognised, in an, at the time, indefinable way, something of the pain and distortion that he was painting. I see the same things every day in the surgery.
>
> And now—you write about the indifference which is crueller than the mutilation and of course that is what I see—people who are absolutely alone with their pain and their fear. And then—and this is where you really help me—you write about the side of the wall which faces the cruelty of life with dignity and flashes of hope—which makes clear that, on the other side, we have ceased to acknowledge the cruelty of life and this denial becomes the essence of loneliness and seems part of the same process which denies the dignity and purpose of dying. You write about the choice on the two sides of the wall being between self-respect and self-chaos—I see them more as being between connection and disconnection—between an aspiration to engage with the totality

[11] Berger, J. *Hold Everything Dear: Dispatches on Survival and Resistance.* Verso, 2007, pp. 85–89.
[12] 5 May 2004.

of human experience or the withholding of engagement. We find hope only on one side of the wall.

And, finally, this brings me back to the experience of being a doctor and the extent of engagement—and about the cost but also the rewards of engagement—in the day—in the night …

On the rich, complacent and lonely side of the medical wall, we deny death and suffering, we view all illness and disease as failure, we see a professional as having technical expertise rather than a vocation, and we value immediate access to doctors above personal continuity of care.

The two sides of the wall in the Bacon paintings and the two sides of the wall within medicine and the society within which it is practiced. I have been intrigued by dualisms throughout my career: object/subject, rich/poor, too much/too little medicine, life/death, public/private, hope/despair, doubt/certainty, and many more. But now, rereading so much of his writing, I realize that John approaches these dualisms in a much more subtle way. I think, for example of his juxtaposition of known/unknown, eternity/immortality, precision/vagueness, silence/seclusion, original/banal, word/story. Some of these seem like opposites and some seem almost to be synonyms but all are to some extent surprising and it is that element of surprise that seems to create a tension within the pairs which opens up each comparison to a much more interesting and fertile ambiguity.

16

MEMORY

In *The Moment of Cubism*, invoking another dualism, John writes:

> Art is concerned with memory: experiment is concerned with pre-
> dictions.[1]

Experiment indicates both science and computing and both are
dedicated to improving the future, all too often at the expense of
the present, as dubious ends continue to justify tawdry means.
Art, all art, is concerned with memory. Within a consultation
the doctor makes use of biomedical science in order to try and
work out if its discoveries can help this particular patient at this
particular moment. At the same time, the patient's stories and
their account of their symptoms are all about memory, their
own and the wider communal memories of family and culture.
The task of bridging these time zones falls to the doctor who
has to cross some very uncertain territory where there are very
few simple answers despite the pretensions of science and policymakers. Whenever we think about time, we should perhaps
ask ourselves again whose time is being given priority here and
now?

[1] Berger, J. 'The Moment of Cubism'. In: *The Sense of Sight*. 1985. Vintage International, 1993, p. 181.

In 2002, I was reading *Keeping a Rendezvous* and John describing:

the three distinct ways in which drawing can function. There are those which study and question the visible, those which put down and communicate ideas, and those done from memory. Even in front of drawings by the old masters, the distinction between the three is important, for each type survives in a different way. Each type of drawing speaks in a different tense. To each we respond with a different capacity of imagination.[2]

I wrote[3] to John in a postscript to another letter:

PS
As usual, if you allow me enough time to catch up, it is you who then hands me the key. This morning, the newspaper arrived late and so I resumed my reading of 'Keeping a Rendezvous' and read about 'Drawing on Paper'. You say that all drawings are either direct studies of life, or they put down an idea or they evoke a memory and that each drawing is in a different tense. But looking again at [your drawing of] Simone Weil, I think I see that it is about both a memory and an idea and that in this way it contains both a possible future and a past. And then thinking on, is it possible that the great Fayum portraits and the ones by Goya touch all three elements and so contain all three dimensions of time—a past and a possible future and a present? Is that their power and our sense of their relevance to the doctor's conversation with the dying patient. And finally, I wonder whether great acting contains all three tenses in the same way?

The following month, I received this immensely encouraging reply:[4]

Your PS, about the Fayum portraits and Goya and (yes, yes) great acting containing all 3 tenses of time is such an insight! And the

---

[2] Berger, J. 'Drawing on Paper'. In *Keeping a Rendezvous*, 1991. Vintage International, 1992, p. 184.
[3] 28 September 2002.
[4] 25 October 2002.

doctor's listening can make the three times co-exist—like at other moments, the stars seem to do.

Also in *Keeping a Rendezvous*, John explained the contradictory nature of memory:

> Memory is a strange faculty. The sharper and more isolated the stimulus memory receives, the more it remembers; the more comprehensive the stimulus, the less it remembers. This is perhaps why black-and-white photography is paradoxically more evocative than colour photography.[5]

This seems true to me and I think of the power of Jean Mohr's black-and-white photographs in *A Fortunate Man* and then I wonder whether this is partly to do with the rarity of back-and-white nowadays, compared with the ubiquity of colour, which makes it more intense.

At the beginning of February 2004, John wrote to me, enclosing a story which he had titled 'The Passeur' and which was later published in his 2005 book *Here Is Where We Meet* as 'Kraków':

> I'm not sure why I want to send you this recent story of mine. I think it has something to do with our dialogues—but I'm not sure how. If it has, you'll see better than me.

At first, I didn't understand quite what he meant but by the time I replied a few days later, I had begun to work it out and I wrote:[6]

> On Thursday, I went to a seminar on 'The hope of a future: refugees in primary care'. A very wise and experienced London

---

[5] Berger, J. 'How Fast Does It Go?' In: *Keeping a Rendezvous*, 1991. Vintage International, 1992, p. 193.
[6] 8 February 2004.

GP talked about the possibility of 100 years of emotional pain being compressed behind a single 10-minute consultation. And he talked about the body expressing a memory that the mind cannot bear to remember. And how telling a story and having it heard connects the 'there' to the 'here'. And then the next morning, your story arrived and I begin to read it and, for me, it is all about the connecting of 'there' to 'here' and the survival of love across both time and distance.

It was all about connecting 'here' to 'there', a theme that John and Giambattista Vico shared throughout their very different lifetimes of writing.

Twenty years earlier, John had written in *Pig Earth*, the first volume of *Into their Labours*:

> In the mountains the past is never behind, it's always to the side. You come down from the forest at dusk and a dog is barking in a hamlet. A century ago in the same spot at the same time of day, a dog, when it heard a man coming down through the forest, was barking, and the interval between the two occasions is no more than a pause in the barking.[7]

And once again, he was connecting 'there' to 'here'. Particularly perhaps in medicine, we always seem to emphasize how much and how rapidly everything about human experience and culture changes, and of course it does, but we tend to forget how much remains almost completely unaltered across millennia: birth, death, injustice, greed, the longing for peace and security, the delight of children, the warmth of the sun, the return of spring, the desire to draw pictures and to make music and so much more. Within medicine, the fear of illness, the life-altering experiences of injury and suffering and the emotional challenge of caring

---

[7] Berger, J. *Pig Earth*, 1979. Chatto & Windus, 1985, p. 163.

for loved others have surely been part of human life for aeons but, tragically, these are just the parts of doctoring that are most neglected in our technocratic age. For me, this is the lesson of the pause in the barking.

I was reading *Here Is Where We Meet* and again, I was thinking and learning about memory. I wrote[8] to John:

> And I have gone on reading—you had already sent me 'Kraków' and 'The Szum and the Ching' but now, of course, I see how powerfully the book makes a whole. You seem to be saying something very important about the link between name and memory. If one has forgotten a name, there is no possibility of meeting—name is somehow fundamental to memory but also, oddly, tangential to it. Much of memory is detached from name but somehow to forget a name is a very fundamental betrayal. I remember many things about my patients and some stories or parts of stories I think I will never forget but I have forgotten many names. Have I understood?

In September 2003, I had serendipitous experience which could only have come my way through John. Simon McBurney, the founder and artistic director of the Théâtre de Complicité, and a very good friend of John's, persuaded me to attend a two-week course taught by two teachers from the famous Paris theatre school founded by Jacques Lecoq. I had to get up very early to see my share of patients before the course began and return to the practice in the evening to catch up again, but these were two extraordinary weeks, during which I had the feeling that I was living a completely different life. Of course, I wrote[9] to John about it:

---

[8] 21 May 2007.
[9] 8 October 2003.

Perhaps the most astounding thing was the work with neutral masks. Have you seen them? You must have done—beautiful leather masks made for Jacques Lecoq—completely expressionless. And the lack of expression means the wearer has no past and no memory—no experience imprinted on the face—and wearing it, you feel alert and receptive and in some odd way innocent—you become a person for whom everything is new—and it seems to me that this state is one that doctors should aspire to—we should try and see patients in this way first—with no preconception, no judgment, no labelling, no memory and only after that first contact return to and use memory and history and the old knowledge.

All too often, working in general practice, a hint from a receptionist or the overheard opinion of another clinician, or a remark, diagnosis, or label put in the medical records, can lead one to prejudge a patient before one has even sat down opposite them in a consulting room. This can be dangerous for both patient and doctor, and I now understand why it is so important to become that person for whom everything is new at that instant.

17

IMAGINATION

In *A Seventh Man*, the 1975 book with Jean Mohr that he financed with half the Booker Prize winnings for his novel *G.*, John could have been speaking directly to doctors:

> To try to understand the experience of another it is necessary to dismantle the world as seen from one's own place within it, and to reassemble it as seen from his. For example, to understand a given choice another makes, one must face in imagination the lack of choices which may confront and deny him. The well-fed are incapable of understanding the choices of the under-fed. The world has to be dismantled and re-assembled in order to be able to grasp, however clumsily, the experience of another. To talk of entering the other's subjectivity is misleading. The subjectivity of another does not simply constitute a different interior attitude to the same exterior facts. The constellation of facts, of which he is the centre, is different.[1]

This dismantling and reassembly demand a deliberate effort of the imagination but I have found the aspiration to achieve this particularly useful when struggling to help those apparently intent on self-destruction: the smoker who simply cannot stop however great the cost to his health, the incorrigibly abusive and violent, the alcoholic at the mercy of his dependence, among

[1] Berger, J. *A Seventh Man*. Penguin Books, 1975, p. 92.

many others. This is difficult for doctors and perhaps even more so within families for those who are trying desperately to cope with a stressed partner or a severely troubled adolescent. In his play *Dublin Carol*, Conor McPherson gives these words to one of his characters who is struggling with alcoholism:

> Sitting on some street corner. Begging for money for drink. You think they don't know it's a short-term solution? They know. But the long term is terrifying. Failure reaching up and grabbing you.

In the essay 'The Place of Painting' in *The Sense of Sight*, John seems to suggest that looking at paintings can nurture the necessary imaginative skills:

> Appearances belong to the boundless space of the visible. With his inner eye man also experiences the space of his own imagination and reflection. . . . Normally it is within the protection of his inner space that man places, retains, cultivates, lets run wild or constructs meaning. At the moment of revelation when appearance and meaning become identical, the space of physics and the seer's inner space coincide: momentarily and exceptionally she or he achieves an equality with the visible. To lose all sense of exclusion; to be at the centre.
>
> The way that all painting, irrespective of its epoch or tradition, interiorizes, brings inside, arranges as a home the visible . . . is a way of safeguarding the experiences of memory and revelation which are man's only defences against that boundless space which otherwise continually threatens to separate and marginalize him.[2]

To me, he seems to be describing the moment when either doctor or patient, or indeed both, experience an epiphany of insight and understanding. This can transform a consultation and a

[2] Berger, J. 'The Place of Painting'. In: *The Sense of Sight*. 1985. Vintage International, 1993, p. 217.

relationship, but just because of its power, it is also dangerous. By its very nature, imagination can lead us to very wrong conclusions and it is always essential to check back repeatedly with the patient and not be led wildly astray and claim understanding that is not real. John warns against this in *A Fortunate Man* when he writes:

> the intimation that the patient should be treated as a total personality, that illness is frequently a form of expression rather than a surrender to natural hazards.
>
> This is dangerous ground, for it is easy to get lost among countless intangibles and to forget or neglect all the precise skills and information which have brought medicine to the point where there is time and opportunity to pursue such intimations.[3]

This doesn't reject the imaginative effort but insists on a firm grasp of biomedical knowledge and reasoning, and on the care and caution that is needed.

In *Keeping a Rendezvous*, John writes that imagination is essential to growth, both as a person and, presumably, as a doctor:

> Birth begins the process of learning to be separate. The separation is hard to believe or accept. Yet, as we accept it, our imagination grows—imagination which is the capacity to reconnect, to bring together that which is separate. Metaphor finds the traces which indicate that all is one. Acts of solidarity, compassion, self-sacrifice, generosity are attempts to re-establish—or at least a refusal to forget—a once-known unity. Death is the hardest test of accepting the separation which life has incurred.[4]

Presumably while still in the process of learning to be separate, John was given a copy of James Joyce's *Ulysses* by a school teacher

3 Berger, J., and Mohr, J. A Fortunate Man. 1967. Penguin Books, 1969, p. 62.
4 Berger, J. Ape Theatre. In Keeping a Rendezvous, 1991. Vintage International 1992, p. 152.

and he read it over the winter of 1940–1941 at the age of fourteen. In his 1991 essay, 'The First and Last Recipe: Ulysses', he credits Joyce with emboldening his imagination:

> Even at my young age, I recognized Joyce's prodigious erudition. He was, in one sense, Learning incarnate. But learning without solemnity that threw away its cap and gown to become joker and juggler. (As I write about him, something of the rhythm of his words still animates my pen.) Perhaps even more significant for me at that time was the company his learning kept: the company of the unimportant, those for ever off stage, the company of publicans and sinners as the Bible puts it, low company. Ulysses is full of the disdain of the represented for those who claim (falsely) to represent them, and packed with the tender ironies of those who are said (falsely) to be lost!
>
> And he did not stop there—this man who was telling me about the life I might never know, this man who never spoke down to anybody, and who remains for me to this day an example of the true adult, which is to say of a being who, because he has accepted life, is intimate with it—this man did not stop there, for his penchant for the lowly led him to keep the same kind of company within his single characters: he listened to their stomachs, their pains, their tumescences: he heard their first impressions, their uncensored thoughts, their ramblings, their prayers without words, their insolent grunts and heaving fantasies. And the more carefully he listened to what scarcely anybody had listened to before, the richer became life's offering.
>
> It was he who showed me, before I knew anything, that literature is inimical to all hierarchies and that to separate fact and imagination, event and feeling, protagonist and narrator, is to stay on dry land and never put to sea.[5]

This clearly suggests that many people have never put to sea, and indeed, that it is not that easy to do so.

---

[5] Published in *Selected Essays by John Berger*, edited by Geoff Dyer, 2001.

Simon McBurney's *Mnemonic* remains the Complicité play that has seemed most important to me as a doctor. I wrote[6] to John:

I found it . . . utterly convincing about the links between memory and imagination—and how each is essential to the other.
The repetitive questions:

'How many mourned him when he disappeared?' 'How many songs did he know?' (Perhaps particularly this one—I don't know why.) 'How many children did he have?' 'What word did he use to signify summer?'[7]

Seem to prove beyond doubt the power of imagination to build links between human beings across extraordinary distances of time and space. And, it all seems to echo Isaiah Berlin writing about Vico,[8]

the central principle which is Vico's ultimate claim to immortality: the principle according to which man can understand himself because, and in the process, of understanding his past—because he is able to reconstruct imaginatively (in Aristotle's phrase) what he did and what he suffered, his hopes, wishes, fears, efforts, his acts and his works, both his own and those of his fellows. With their experience his own is interwoven, his own and his (and their) ancestors', whose monuments, customs, laws, but above all words, still speak to him; indeed, if they did not, and if he did not understand them, he would not understand his fellows' or his own symbols, he would not be able to communicate or think or conceive purposes, to form societies or become fully human.[9]

---

[6] 11 February 2001.

[7] Complicité. *Mnemonic*. Methuen Publishing, 2001.

[8] Giovanni Battista Vico (1668–1744) spent most of his professional life as Professor of Rhetoric at the University of Naples. His highly original views are most fully expressed in his mature work, the *Scienza Nuova*. https://plato.stanford.edu/archives/fall2022/entries/vico/

[9] Berlin, I. *Against the Current: Essays in the History of Ideas.* 1979. Pimlico, 1997, p. 114.

Sometimes when a consultation feels stuck, there is a need to jolt the conversation by asking a question that seems to have almost nothing to do with medicine but which often has the power to reveal information of great relevance and which allows the doctor to see the patient in a completely different light. The repetitive questions in *Mnemonic* are just that sort of question.

In his novel *King*, John wrote:

> [Giambattista Vico] believed the word humanitas came from the verb humare, to bury. The burying of the dead is what he meant. Man's humanity, according to him, began with a respect for the dead.[10]

And I wonder about the effects of the contemporary denial of death and the cultural isolation of the dying on the nature of our humanity, and perhaps particularly the way we have allowed the rituals of funeral and mourning to be subverted into 'the celebration of a life' which does almost nothing to reflect the desperate realities of loss and grief.

[10] Berger, J. *King: A Street Story*. 1999. Vintage International, 2000, p. 85.

18

PAIN

For me, pain is a symptom which always has the power to make me feel inadequate as a doctor because it so inaccessible. I have been helped because John wrote a lot about pain. In *Pig Earth*, John touches on this inaccessibility:

> Pleasure is always your own, and it varies as much and no more than pain does.[1]

He wrote[2] me a letter about pain:

> On the last day of the haymaking, lifting the hay too abruptly, I pulled my back and now have a chronic lumbago. [2½ minutes to getup from a chair!] Nothing to worry about, it's now being treated—anti-inflammatory injections and the lot. I only tell you this because I've spent a lot of time lying on my back, vaguely chatting in my mind about pain.
>
> Of course there are as many pains as situations and people. And of course physical and psychic intertwine to make the pain. But I saw one thing (perhaps) which hadn't occurred to me before. There are destructive pains and there are confirming pains. The latter not necessarily less intense. The confirming pains come from the body re-stabilising itself after a trauma. The destructive pains speak for themselves. The confirming ones (oddly) positively <u>increase</u>

[1] Berger, J. *Pig Earth*, 1979. Chatto & Windus, 1985, p. 186.
[2] 13 August 2001.

confidence, leading to a sense of invulnerablility—very close to
that which can be experienced after orgasm! And this, I'm certain,
has nothing to do with sado-masochism. It feels almost chemical.
A passive erotic pain? Close to the sensation of being desired.

When a skilled writer analyses and writes about a symptom, it
almost always helps to increase the doctor's understanding of
that symptom. The detail of the description is a gift. I had never
thought about the possibility of confirming pains but I am now
familiar with them from personal experience and I know how
reassuring they can be.

In *Keeping a Rendezvous*, in his essay 'A Story for Aesop', he wrote:

> Anatomy for him [Goya] is a vain, rationalist exercise that has noth-
> ing to do with the savagery and suffering of our bodies.[3]

And here, we have, very precisely, the contrast between the objective biomedical gaze and the empathic intersubjective gaze that
a doctor must attempt to bridge. There is a requirement to see
and explore the anatomy but any knowledge derived in this way
is fatally weakened without an effort to understand each patient's
experience of the suffering enclosed within that anatomy. I am
reminded of a patient, a young man, a refugee from war, who
had disabling pain in his leg which meant that he had to walk
with a stick. The objective anatomical gaze of both doctors and
machines could find nothing wrong in the leg but this man had
been tortured and his knee had somehow been a focus of his torture and his pain was its almost inevitable legacy that demanded
to be acknowledged and respected.

---

[3] Berger, J. 'A Story for Aesop'. In: *Keeping a Rendezvous*, 1991. Vintage International, 1992,
p. 75.

In the second paragraph of his novel *G.*, John wrote:

> When she was twenty-one her father died suddenly. The mystery of her own poor health began with his death and gradually established the foundations of a lifelong right: the right to be less than present, the right to withdraw.[4]

Biography has the power to scar biological health, often irremediably.

In *And Our Faces*, John emphasized this with a question:

> The emotional pain of loss, the pain that has broken a heart. Such pain fills the space of an entire life. It may have begun with a single event but the event has produced a surplus of pain. The sufferer becomes inconsolable. Yet, what is this pain, if it is not the recognition that what was once given as pleasure or happiness has been irrevocably taken away?[5]

John finds accounts of this arena of pain in the work, not only of Goya, but of many other Spanish painters including Ribera, Zubarán, Murillo, and Velazquez. Returning to *Keeping a Rendezvous*, we find:

> What makes Spanish painting Spanish is that in it is to be discovered the same anguish as the landscapes of the great *mesa* of the interior often provoked on those who lived and worked among them.[6]

And John then quoted the Spanish philosopher Miguel de Unamuno:

---

[4] Berger, J. *G.* 1972. Bloomsbury Publishing, 1996, p. 3.
[5] Berger, J. *And Our Faces, My Heart, Brief as Photos.* 1984. Vintage International, 1991, p. 71.
[6] Berger, J. 'A Story for Aesop'. In: *Keeping a Rendezvous.* 1991. Vintage International, 1992, p. 77.

Suffering is, in effect, the barrier which unconsciousness, matter, sets up against consciousness, spirit; it is the resistance to will, the limit which the visible universe imposes upon God.[7]

The savagery of the visible universe all too easily becomes intractable pain.

In *A Fortunate Man*, John wrote about the relationship of anguish to loss:

> Anguish arises from a sense of irreparable loss. This loss is added to all the other losses sustained during one's life: these other losses represent the absence of what one might otherwise have turned to for consolation on the occasion of this one, the most recent and final of all.[8]

And he explores the complex interface between anguish and time, with time having the capacity to exacerbate anguish unbearably:

> Anguish has its own time-scale. What separates the anguished person from the unanguished is a barrier of time: a barrier which intimidates the imagination of the latter.[9]
>
> . . .
>
> The anguished are trapped in a moment which is born of all that has happened to them. Faced with the irreversibility of events—so terrible for all who are unprepared, and none can be fully prepared—it is their experience which bends in a circle: unable to catch time by the tail, they chase their own, revolving in one moment blindly through all their life. How much then can a moment contain?[10]

[7] de Unamuno, Miguel. *Tragic Sense of Life*, trans. J. E. Crawford Flitch, 1921. Dover Publications, 1954, p. 212.

[8] Berger, J., and Mohr, J. *A Fortunate Man*. 1967. Penguin Books, 1969, p. 123.

[9] Berger, J., and Mohr, J. *A Fortunate Man*. 1967. Penguin Books, 1969, p. 113.

[10] Berger, J., and Mohr, J. *A Fortunate Man*. 1967. Penguin Books, 1969, p. 127.

And somehow, behind pain and suffering, death is always lurk-
ing. When pain destroys happiness, it seems to waste life itself and
make death even more threatening:

> All doctors are more than usually aware of death . . . In the human
> imagination death and the passing of time are indissolubly linked:
> each moment that passes brings us nearer to our death: and our
> death, if it can be measured at all, is measured by that apparent
> eternity of existence which must continue after and without us.[11]

As we have already heard, John experienced a lot of pain himself,
most particularly, as a result of his recurrent back problems. John
wrote[12] to me:

> It's nothing really—but it distracts one's confidence—which you
> need so much of, no?—if you try to think and travel outwards. The
> best is on my motor-bike (!)—then either it stops, or I'm so engaged
> in movement and thrust that I leave it behind! I tell you all this—a
> little with tongue in cheek—because it's another way of trying to
> name a living-with-something.

A few days later, I replied:[13]

> I shouldn't minimise the potential of your motor-bike to help you
> leave the pain behind—healing as the recovery of the ability to for-
> get?

[11] Berger, J., and Mohr, J. A Fortunate Man. 1967. Penguin Books, 1969, p. 126.
[12] 14 November 2000.
[13] 19 November 2000.

19

VIOLENCE

In the opening paragraph of his essay 'The White Bird', John wrote:

> The problem is that you can't talk about aesthetics without talking about the principle of hope and the existence of evil.[1]

And, for me, this is really a manifesto for his life's work. Unlike so many who write about art, often with great sensitivity and erudition, John was never content with the easy or the superficial, however beautiful. He never lost sight of the centuries of violence that underpin so much European culture and he insisted that this violence should be acknowledged. In *The Look of Things*, he described

> the world-historical moment at which we have arrived. Imperialism, European hegemony, the moralities of capitalist-Christianity and state communism, the Cartesian dualism of white reasoning, the practice of constructing 'humanist' cultures on a basis of monstrous exploitation.[2]

This violent history, which seems to become worse with every passing year, also lurked within my consulting room where I, a

---

[1] Berger, J. 'The White Bird'. In: *The Sense of Sight*. 1985. Vintage International, 1993, p. 5.
[2] Berger, J. *Selected Essays and Articles: The Look of Things*. Penguin Books, 1972, p. 203.

privileged white woman, presumed to understand the displaced, the impoverished, the frightened, and the fleeing. Somehow, I need to acknowledge and respect this history within my daily practice but it is not an easy path to tread without being crass or condescending. I think that just being aware of the burden of historical guilt that I carry must help somehow to keep me on the narrow path I have set myself.

At the beginning of *G.*, John described a crowd:

> Such a crowd is a solemn test of a man. . . . It has assembled to demand the impossible. It has assembled to avenge the discrepancy. Its need to overthrow the order which has defined and distinguished between the possible and the impossible at its expense, for generation after generation. In face of such a crowd there are only two ways in which a man, who is not already of it, can react. Either he sees in it the hope of mankind or else he fears it absolutely.[3]

This particular crowd is making a political protest but the same polarization can be applied to a crowd anywhere, in an art gallery or even in a general practice waiting room. In all these places we seek the hope of humanity in the assembled crowd. We may not always find it but we should look for it nonetheless.

I find more guidance in *A Fortunate Man*:

> There is a strict frontier between moral examples and the use of force. Once pushed over that frontier, survival depends upon chance. All those who have never been pushed that far are, by definition, fortunate and will question the truth of the world's brute indifference. All who have been forced across the frontier—even if they survive and return—recognize different functions, different substances in the most basic materials—in metal, wood, earth,

[3] Berger, J. *G.* 1972. Bloomsbury Publishing, 1996, p. 10.

stone, as also in the human mind and body. Do not become too subtle. The privilege of being subtle is the distinction between the fortunate and the unfortunate.[4]

And I am reminded that:

It is the nature of this world that good wishes and noble protests seldom mitigate between the blow and the pain. For most of those who suffer, there is no appeal.

All modalities of violence wound and scar body and mind simultaneously. Years ago, I attended a meeting at the then Department of Health alongside a group of women who were living with chronic and enduring mental illness. These women argued that mental illness of this severity was caused by child sexual abuse until proved otherwise. This lived insight was to be enormously helpful to me, and I hope to my patients, over the succeeding years.

It is no surprise that John had anticipated my discovery when he wrote in *A Fortunate Man*:

With the fatal a-historical basis of our culture, we tend to overlook or ignore the historical content of neuroses or mental illness.[5]

The American medical anthropologist Nancy Scheper-Hughes defines structural violence as

violence that is permissible, even encouraged. It refers to the invisible social machinery of inequality that reproduces social relations of exclusion and marginalization via ideologies, stigmas, and dangerous discourses attendant to race, class, sex, and other invidious distinctions. Structural violence 'naturalizes' poverty,

[4] Berger, J., and Mohr, J. *A Fortunate Man*. 1967. Penguin Books, 1969, p. 134.
[5] Berger, J., and Mohr, J. *A Fortunate Man*. 1967. Penguin Books, 1969, p. 144.

sickness, hunger, and premature death, erasing their social and political origins so that they are taken for granted and no one is held accountable except the poor themselves.[6]

I wrote[7] to John:

> Maria [Nadotti] wants me to write another book[8] so I am beginning to toy with that idea. I think it could be about the connections between sorrow and sickness taking in the debilitating nature of loss—of love or hope or place or story—and the possibility of redress through story, relationship, attention, detail, listening. The way the pursuit of capitalist profit drives the structural violence that makes the poor sick and, as health becomes more and more commodified and healthcare more commercialised, the way in which the same pursuit of profit dictates the way sickness is conceptualised and treated. And also wondering why—so often—politicians seem to hate doctors. Clearly, I have a lot more thinking to do!

General practitioners witness, at first hand, political priorities playing out in the lives of ordinary people and their experience has much to tell us about what is wrong with society and state policy. We have a responsibility to speak out, to speak truth to power, whenever we have an opportunity.

As John wrote in *A Fortunate Man*:

> Vulnerability may have its own private causes, but it often reveals concisely what is wounding and damaging on a much larger scale.[9]

---

[6] Scheper-Hughes, N. 'Dangerous and Endangered Youth: Social Structures and Determinants of Violence'. *Annals of the New York Academy of Sciences*, 2004, 1036: 13–46.

[7] 13 March 2013.

[8] The book was eventually published in 2016 in an Italian translation by Maria Nadotti as *Contro il Mercato della Salute*.

[9] Berger, J., and Mohr, J. *A Fortunate Man*. 1967. Penguin Books, 1969, p. 144.

In 1988, John contributed to a conversation in photographer Chris Killip's great book *In Flagrante* which portrayed the grotesque structural violence that remains the enduring legacy of Margaret Thatcher:

In the sky, beyond every photograph in this book, is reflected the blind indifference of the new individualism. Finally history will not forgive this indifference. Meanwhile in its monstrous light something else becomes visible.

When the first factories and mines were built in the North of England and Scotland, when the first proletariat ever created, surged in and out of the iron gates, before barbed-wire had been invented, and, a little later, when Engels and Mayhew made their pioneer voyages of horrified discovery, the world of 'the labouring classes' was thought of as an underworld, its inhabitants sub-human, their impulses 'animal', their fates unknowable yet nevertheless the issue of unnameable sins!

Many of the terms used to describe this underworld were borrowed from those which had been used to justify the slave trade, whose profits had supplied the first capital for launching the new industries.

Today theoreticians of the New Right denigrate the written-off in a similar spirit. The epithets may have changed, but not the principle whereby they explain that the wretchedness they themselves impose is the consequence of the moral debility of the 'wretched'.

What has become visible and obvious is that this is a lie. This first equality *has* been won. It confers no protection, guarantees no rights. It simply recognises that those living today in the zones of abandonment differ in no essential way from anybody else.[10]

[10] Berger, J., and Grant, S. 'Walking back Home'. In: Killip, C. In Flagrante. 1988. Martin Secker & Warburg Ltd, pp. 85–93.

And this reminds me of the smouldering anger of the young radical poet Percy Bysshe Shelley, writing more than two hundred years earlier:

> The rich grind the poor into abjectness and then complain that they are abject.[11]

Homelessness is perhaps the most shameful expression of society's structural violence. When I first joined my practice in 1975, we provided care to the residents of Arlington House in Camden Town which was, at that time, the largest hostel for single men in Europe. The rooms were tiny and the regime punitively harsh. The stories these men told were full of violence, physical and emotional, alongside structural, and were immeasurably sad. And in this context, as John wrote in *A Fortunate Man*:

> The notion of endurance is fundamentally far more important than happiness.[12]

The men I got to know and respect revealed a capacity for endurance in the face of abuse, violence, poverty, and much more that often seemed to me to be unsurvivable.

In *And Our Faces* John wrote:

> To the underprivileged, home is represented, not by a house, but by a practice or set of practices. Everyone has his own. These practices, chosen and not imposed, offer in their repetition, transient as they may be in themselves, more permanence, more shelter than any lodging. Home is no longer a dwelling but the untold story of

---

[11] Jones, F. L. (ed). The Letters of Percy Bysshe Shelley, 1964. Oxford University Press, Volume 1, No. 174, p. 271.
[12] Berger, J., and Mohr, J. A Fortunate Man. 1967. Penguin Books, 1969, p. 134.

a life being lived. At its most brutal, home is no more than one's name—whilst to most people one is nameless.[13]

And:

The roof over the head, the four walls, have become, as it were secular: independent from whatever is kept in the heart and is sacred. Such secularization is the direct consequence of economic and social conditions: tenancy, poverty, overcrowding, city planning, property speculation. But ultimately it is the consequence of a lack of choice. Without a history of choice no dwelling can be a home.[14]

[13] Berger, J. *And Our Faces, My Heart, Brief as Photos.* 1984. Vintage International, 1991, p. 64.
[14] Berger, J. *And Our Faces, My Heart, Brief as Photos.* 1984. Vintage International, 1991, pp. 63–64.

20

JUSTICE AND SOLIDARITY

After his visit to Palestine in 2006, John wrote:

> The worst cruelties of life are its killing injustices. Almost all promises are broken. The poor's acceptance of adversity is neither passive nor resigned.[1]

His commitment to justice and solidarity ran like a river through all his writing. He found everyone worthy of attention and had no patience with those who would allocate different status to different people. I do not know where this commitment came from but nonetheless it is always present and always palpable.

I share John's preoccupation with justice which, I think in my case, dates from events in my childhood that have to do with shame, but which has undoubtedly been consolidated by my experience of trying to care for the huge diversity of people on the losing side of injustice, who I sat and listened to in inner London general practice. This probably explains why, over the years, I have copied out so many of John's sentences that tackle the issues of justice and solidarity.

---

[1] Berger, J. 'Dispatches: Undefeated Despair'. Race & Class. 2006, 48(1): 33.

I wrote[2] to John:

> Your association of the snot of a common cold with a sense of
> shame is fascinating. We know that psychological stress lowers the
> body's immunity and increases the incidence of minor infections
> including the common cold. And Richard Wilkinson, who has
> done all the work to show that health inequalities in the developed
> world are driven by relative rather than absolute poverty, has
> come to think that a sense of shame is the key to understanding
> what is happening. There seems to be a process by which poverty
> produces a sense of insecurity and loss of self-esteem, which in
> turn creates chronic psychosocial stress and, through associated
> physiological changes, particularly on the immune system, comes
> to be transformed into disease. When two good people use the
> same word there must be something in it!

My understanding of the pervasiveness of shame and its possible
relationship to my own commitment to justice dates back to my
parents' acrimonious divorce in the 1950s. I never told any of my
school friends about it and, although I went to stay with many of
them, I never invited them back. I think that, without understanding it, I had picked up on my mother's sense of shame (divorce was
very stigmatizing in the 1950s). Years later, I was involved in orga-
nizing a conference about health inequalities and we all went up
to wherever it was the night before and ate supper together. One
of our number suggested that there must be some biographical
reason why we were each concerned about social justice. My own
explanation was that I had learned early on that one can assume a
burden of shame through no fault of one's own. I don't know but I
think that John's commitment may have come by quite a different
route: through years of listening carefully and thinking deeply.

---

[2] 6 December 2000.

Writing in *Studio International* in 1983, John explained why he felt such an affinity to Caravaggio:

> The few canvases from my own incomparably modest life as a painter, which I would like to see again, are those I painted in the late 40s of the streets of Livorno. This city was then war-scarred and poor, and it was there that I first began to learn something about the ingenuity of the dispossessed. It was there too that I discovered that I wanted as little as possible to do in this world with those who wield power. This has turned out to be a life-long aversion.[3]

I wrote[4] to John:

> Yesterday, I went to a seminar at the London School of Economics which was meant to be about socio-economic inequalities in the care of older people but seemed mostly to be about sophisticated mathematical modelling of patients' movements in and out of hospital—which in its way expresses everything that is wrong about the way we treat old people. But there was one wonderful contribution from Malcolm Johnson who is an Emeritus Professor of Social Policy from Bristol. He spoke about the public policy tradition in Britain whereby a person may only benefit from the public purse if they are to some extent humiliated.
>
> He also described how, in rich countries, the concurrence of old age and death is now much stronger than ever before in human history with 80% of deaths taking place over the age of 65. I wondered whether the increasingly shabby treatment of frail old people is, in some way, part of the contemporary denial of death.
>
> But the best things that he said were about an idea of bio- graphical pain which is entwined in the losses and failures of

---

[3] Berger, J. 'Caravaggio: A Contemporary View'. *Studio International.* 1983, 196(998). https://www.studiointernational.com/caravaggio-a-contemporary-view-by-john-berger-vol-196-no-998-1983.

[4] 9 April 2003.

life. He defined it as 'the irremediable anguish which results from profoundly painful recollection of experienced wrongs which can now never be righted—when finitude or impairment terminates the possibility of cherished self-promises to redress deeply regretted action'.

The minute he said it, it was instantly recognisable but I have never heard these very common things expressed quite that way before and, as always, new words are helpful. And he went on to talk about contemporary spiritual illiteracy which means that we have no way of talking about regret and forgiveness and I wondered whether our spiritual illiteracy was also directly related to our need to deny the value of pain. I think that you can see that in a day that was mostly about reducing people to data in a mathematical model this talk shone like a beacon!

In his 1964 novel *Corker's Freedom*, John wrote:

This is why life is so dangerous. We are surrounded by stupidities we must accept as though they made sense and by mistakes we must count on being made. No appeal to justice can ever save a faller: all that can save him is being forewarned: he must know that stupidity is certain, that injustice is bound to be done, that truth waits to be travestied.[5]

Twenty years later, in *Pig Earth*, he wrote:

Both the bourgeois and Marxist ideals of equality presume a world of plenty; they demand equal rights for all before a cornucopia, a cornucopia to be constructed by science and the advancement of knowledge. What the two understand by equal rights is of course very different. The peasant ideal of equality recognizes a world of scarcity, and its promise is for mutual fraternal aid in struggling against this scarcity and a just sharing of what the work

[5] Berger, J. *Corker's Freedom*. 1964. Writers and Readers Publishing Cooperative, 1979, p. 108.

produces. Closely connected with the peasant's recognition, as a survivor, of scarcity, is his recognition of man's relative ignorance. He may admire knowledge and the fruits of knowledge but he never supposes that the advance of knowledge reduces the extent of the unknown. This non-antagonistic relation between the unknown and knowing explains why some of his knowledge is accommodated in what, from the outside, is defined as superstition and magic. Nothing in his experience encourages him to believe in final causes, precisely because his experience is so wide. The unknown can only be eliminated within the limits of a laboratory experiment. Those limits seem to him to be naïve.[6]

Despite the unprecedented wealth of a tiny minority, the vast majority of the world's population, even within the richest countries, continues the ancestral struggle against scarcity. The experience of this struggle with its continual stress and insecurity, undermines health and eventually plays out in premature death. General practitioners know many of those who struggle and they see at first-hand the price they pay. Too many governments and policymakers seem to think that the resulting health problems can be treated with medication validated within the limits of laboratory experiment. Nothing could be more naïve.

In spring 2005, during the *John Berger: Here Is Where We Meet* season in London, David and I attended an exhibition and a discussion of photographs by Mehmet Emir which documented the experiences of his father as a Turkish (Kurdish) guestworker in Vienna. It was held in the elegant surroundings of the Austrian Cultural Forum in Rutland Gate and we noticed that many in the audience were holding their, by then, thirty-year-old paperback copies of *A Seventh Man*, John's second book with Jean Mohr. I

---

[6] Berger, J. *Pig Earth*, 1979. Chatto & Windus, 1985, p. 202.

am ashamed to remember that, at that time, I had not even read *A Seventh Man*.

In his Booker Prize acceptance speech, John said this about *A Seventh Man*:

> G. took five years to write. Since then I have been planning the next five years of my life. I have begun a project about the migrant workers of Europe. I do not know what form the final book will take. Perhaps a novel. Perhaps a book that fits no category. What I do know is that I want some of the voices of the eleven million migrant workers in Europe and of the forty or so million that are their families, mostly left behind in towns and villages but dependent on the wages of the absent worker, to speak through the pages of this book. Poverty forces the migrants, year after year, to leave their own places and culture and come to do much of the dirtiest and worst paid work in the industrialized areas of Europe, where they form the reserve army of labour. What is their view of the world? Of themselves? Of us? Of their own exploitation?[7]

A Seventh Man was published in 1975 and, in it, John wrote:

> If he lives austerely, he can still save or send home £150 a month. With these savings he imagines he is transforming his own life and his family's. Working in the tunnel, each man is more or less locked in his personal vision of a better future. This adds to the isolation caused by language. It can lead, sometimes, to a kind of negligence—of the present and of the self.[8]

Looking forward to the destroyed lives that Chris Killip documented in the north-east of England under Margaret Thatcher, and the populist racist rhetoric indulged by right-wing politicians around Brexit, John wrote:

[7] https://thebookerprizes.com/the-booker-library/features/i-have-to-turn-the-prize-against-itself-john-bergers-1972-booker-prize
[8] Berger, J. *A Seventh Man*. Penguin Books, 1975, p. 163.

Equality has nothing to do with capacity or function: it is a recognition of being. . . .

This is why the working class, if it accepts the natural inferiority of the migrants, is likely to reduce its own demands to economic ones, to fragment itself and to lose its own political identity. When the indigenous worker accepts inequality as the principle to sustain his own self-esteem, he reinforces and completes the fragmentation which society is already imposing upon him.[9]

In *And Our Faces*, John wrote: 'In reality many [problems] are insoluble—hence the never-ending need for solidarity.'[10]

I wrote[11] to John:

We managed to track down a copy of *A Seventh Man* and I have been reading it and it tells the story of so many of my displaced patients. And this morning there is news of one man dying and one man being terribly burnt in an accident in the building of the new Channel Tunnel rail link tunnel to Kings' Cross and I wonder about the stories of those men. You write about how the dream of a better future can lead to 'a kind of negligence—of the present and of the self' and it seems to me that, since you wrote it, this kind of negligence has become a kind of global epidemic with everyone driving towards a different future and almost not noticing the present—with no time for Anne Michaels' 'looking in order to remember' and no time for Patrick Kavanagh's 'passionate transitory'.

At the beginning you write about unfreedom: 'This unfreedom can only be fully recognised if an objective economic system is related to the subjective experience of those trapped within it. Indeed, finally, the unfreedom is that relationship.'

In his essay *Erasing the Past*, John forges the connection between justice and medicine through Chekhov:

[9] Berger, J. *A Seventh Man*. Penguin Books, 1975, p. 141.
[10] Berger J. *And Our Faces, My Heart, Brief as Photos*. 1984. Vintage International, 1991, p. 67.
[11] 17 August 2005.

I recall a sentence by Anton Chekhov, who was also a doctor. 'The role of the writer is to describe a situation so truthfully . . . that the reader can no longer evade it'. We today with our lived historical experiences, which the political machines are trying to erase, have to be both that reader and writer . . . it's within our power.[12]

Yet, in *A Fortunate Man*, he had already made the connection very clear, when he wrote:

> There are occasions when any doctor may feel helpless: faced with a tragic incurable disease; faced with obstinacy and prejudice maintaining the very situation which has created the illness or unhappiness; faced with certain housing conditions; faced with poverty.[13]

And, most immediately, when he asks the burning question, to which I have never found an answer:

> How much right have we to go on being always patient on behalf of others?[14]

When I wrote[15] to John, he had been visiting Palestine:

> She [Maria Nadotti] sent me her photograph of you and Melina [John's granddaughter] walking by that terrible wall—it is an extraordinary photo—such a shocking juxtaposition of love and atrocity. . . . It occurs to me that walking by the wall is what you have done with your life—coming close to atrocity, witnessing it and writing about it, but never losing sight of love and courage and endurance.
>
> There is a very good article in *The Guardian* today—by Terry Waite—asking 'Were my captors worse than the Guantánamo

[12] https://www.spokesmanbooks.com/Spokesman/PDF/97Berger.pdf
[13] Berger, J., and Mohr, J. *A Fortunate Man*. 1967. Penguin Books, 1969, p. 132.
[14] Berger, J., and Mohr, J. *A Fortunate Man*. 1967. Penguin Books, 1969, p. 133.
[15] 23 November 2005.

jailers?"[16] and being absolutely clear that the answer is no—he writes:

> Our connivance with the war against Iraq is linked with the shallowness of thought that appears to be part of parliamentary decision-making. It seems decisions are taken without any concern for the long-term consequences.

On Friday, I have to go to Walsall to talk at a conference on racism in healthcare and I will try to discuss the shallowness of thought—the hypocrisy of the mixed messages of inclusion and equity within healthcare contrasted with the demonisation of refugees and asylum-seekers and the desperately destructive abolition of civil rights in the name of fighting 'terrorism'.

Figure 8 Melina and John Berger in Qalkilya, West Bank, 30 October 2005. On the wall that separates Palestine from Israel one reads: 'To exist is to resist'.
Source: Photo by Maria Nadotti. Reproduced with permission.

[16] https://www.theguardian.com/world/2005/nov/23/terrorism.politics

In his essay about Palestine, published in *Race & Class*, John wrote:

> On this earth, there is no happiness without a longing for justice.
> Happiness is not something to be pursued, it is something met, an encounter. Most encounters, however, have a sequel; this is their promise. The encounter with happiness has no sequel. All is there instantly. Happiness is what pierces grief.[17]

John wrote a lot about promise and I think it is his way of describing the persistence, but also the fragility of hope, in the face of the active perpetuation of injustice and structural violence.

In *Hold Everything Dear*, John quoted Walter Benjamin:

> In the mid-twentieth century Walter Benjamin wrote: 'The state of emergency in which we live is not the exception but the rule. We must attain to a concept of history that is in keeping with this insight.'
> Within such a concept of history we have come to see that every simplification, every label, serves only the interests of those who wield power; the more extensive their power, the greater their need for simplifications. And, by contrast, the interests of those who suffer under, or struggle against this blind power, are served now and for the long, long future by the recognition and acceptance of diversity, differences and complexities.[18]

This underlines the banality and empty hypocrisy of the use of words in so many of the policymaking documents that I was expected to read, compared with the baffling complexities of the lives that so many are obliged to lead.

---

[17] Berger, J. 'Dispatches: Undefeated Despair'. Race & Class. 2006, 48(1): 33.
[18] Berger, J. *Hold Everything Dear: Dispatches on Survival and Resistance*. Verso, 2007, p. 134.

21

FEAR

John died in January 2017 and, although the world has felt a much smaller and less generous place since then, I find myself glad that he did not have to live through that terrible combination of fear and competitive authoritarianism that marked the first two years of the Covid 19 pandemic. Yet, in a way, he had already written about Covid when he contemplated HIV-AIDS in his beautiful novel *To the Wedding* from 1995:

> We're living on the brink, and it's hard because we've lost the habit. Once everybody, old and young, rich and poor, took it for granted. Life was painful and precarious. Chance was cruel. On feast days there were brioches.
>
> For two centuries we've believed in history as a highway which was taking us to a future such as nobody had ever known before. We thought we were exempt. When we walked through the galleries of the old palaces and saw all those massacres and last rites and decapitated heads on platters, all painted and framed on the walls, we told ourselves we had come a long way—not so far that we couldn't still feel for them, of course, but far enough to know we'd been spared. Now people live to be much older. There are anaesthetics. We've landed on the moon. There are no more slaves. We apply reason to everything. Even to Salome dancing. We forgave the past its errors because they occurred in the Dark Ages. Now, suddenly we find ourselves far from any highway, perched like puffins on a cliff edge in the dark.[1]

---

[1] Berger, J. *To the Wedding*. 1995. Bloomsbury Publishing, 1996, pp. 148–149.

Reading this again in 2023, it feels even more relevant to Covid than it did to HIV-AIDS because back in the 1980s it was mostly gay men and people from Africa who found themselves perched on the cliff edge in the dark and overwhelmed by fear. In 2020 and 2021, the fear was felt by everyone even though, as always, structural violence exerted its usual malign effect with those on the losing side finding themselves at much greater risk.

Much of John's wisdom came from what he saw in paintings and what he learnt from them and he showed me how it was possible to see and learn much more than I had ever imagined possible. In *Keeping a Rendezvous*, John described what he saw in the eyes of Goya portraits, especially when the painter was painting his friends:

> If you place these portraits side by side, a curious thing becomes evident: their eyes have the same expression: an unflinching, lucid resignation—as if they had already seen the unspeakable, as if the existent could no longer surprise them and was scarcely worth observing any more.[2]

I recognize this expression and I have seen it in the eyes of many of my patients who have lived through fear and become resigned to the imminence of death. If it can be achieved, it seems a good state in which to confront death.

Fear, sometimes very well hidden, is present within almost every general practice consultation, however trivial the complaint appears to be. Any patient may think that what they are experiencing predicts some appalling future: loss of life, capacity, independence, and much else. In *A Fortunate Man*, John explained

[2] Berger, J. 'A Story for Aesop'. In: *Keeping a Rendezvous*. 1985. Vintage International, 1992, p. 73.

very clearly how fear can only be contained and, at least to some extent, relieved if the patient feels themselves to be seen in all the detail of our individuality:

> This individual and closely intimate recognition is required on both a physical and psychological level. On the former it constitutes the art of diagnosis. Good general diagnosticians are rare, not because most doctors lack medical knowledge, but because most are incapable of taking in all the possibly relevant facts—emotional, historical, environmental as well as physical. They are searching for specific conditions instead of the truth about a man which may then suggest various conditions. . . .

> On the psychological level recognition means support. As soon as we are ill we fear that our illness is unique. We argue with ourselves and rationalize, but a ghost of the fear remains. And it remains for a very good reason. The illness, as an undefined force, is a potential threat to our very being and we are bound to be highly conscious of the uniqueness of that being. The illness, in other words, shares in our own uniqueness. By fearing its threat, we embrace it and make it specially our own. That is why patients are inordinately relieved when doctors give their complaints a name. The name may mean very little to them; they understand nothing of what it signifies; but because it has a name, it has an independent existence from them. They can now struggle or complain against it. To have a complaint recognised, that is to say defined, limited and depersonalized, is to be made stronger.[3]

Yet it is not only the patient but also the doctor who brings fear into the consulting room. All doctors, especially when working in under-resourced settings, bring at least some small burden of fear: fear of making a mistake, fear of missing something, and perhaps particularly, fear of failing their patients. John used the word

[3] Berger, J., and Mohr, J. A Fortunate Man. 1967. Penguin Books, 1969, pp.73–74.

anguish and I think he was using it to combine the sensations of pain with those of fear, which, so often, coalesce in a single feeling. He asks:

> What is the effect of facing, trying to understand, hoping to overcome the extreme anguish of other persons five or six times a week? I do not speak of physical anguish, for that can usually be relieved in a matter of minutes. I speak of the anguish of dying, of loss, of fear, of loneliness, of being desperately beside oneself, of the sense of futility.[4]

Here I think John may have overestimated the extent to which the physical can be separated from the other modalities of anguish and underestimated how often they overlap and, when I find myself thinking this, I am suddenly aware of how much I miss the opportunity of being able to write to him about this more than it is possible for me to express.

---

[4] Berger, J., and Mohr, J. *A Fortunate Man*. 1967. Penguin Books, 1969, p. 113.

22

DOUBT

The American physicist Richard P. Feynman gave a public address entitled *The Value of Science* at the 1955 autumn
meeting of the National Academy of Sciences. He said:

> The scientist has a lot of experience with ignorance and doubt
> and uncertainty, and this experience is of very great importance,
> I think. When a scientist doesn't know the answer to a problem,
> he is ignorant. When he has a hunch about what the result is
> going to be, he is uncertain. And when he is pretty darn sure of
> what the result is going to be, he is still in some doubt. We have
> found it of paramount importance that in order to progress we
> must recognize our ignorance and leave room for doubt. Scientific
> knowledge is a body of statements of varying degrees of certainty—
> some most unsure, some nearly sure, but none absolutely
> certain.
>
> Now, we scientists are used to this, and we take it for granted that
> it is perfectly consistent to be unsure, that it is possible to live and
> not know. But I don't know whether everyone realizes this is true.
> Our freedom to doubt was born out of a struggle against authority
> in the early days of science. It was a very deep and strong struggle:
> permit us to question—to doubt—to not be sure. I think it is impor-
> tant that we do not forget this struggle and thus perhaps lose what
> we have gained. Herein lies a responsibility to society.[1]

[1] Feynman, R. P., as told to Ralph Leighton. 'The Value of Science'. In: *What Do You Care What Other People Think?* 1988. Harper Collins, 1993, p. 245

Sadly, I read this after John had died because I would love to have discussed it with him and to have lamented the deeply regrettable pandemic usage of 'Follow the Science' to imply a certainty which, at the time, was entirely absent.

I think John would have understood because in *A Fortunate Man* he quotes John Sassall as saying:

> 'You never know *for certain* about anything. This sounds falsely modest and trite, but it's the honest truth. Most of the time you are right and you do *appear* to know, but every now and then the rules seem to get broken and then you realize how lucky you have been on the occasions when *you think you have known* and have been proved correct.'[2]

This is exactly how I have felt on so many occasions. For a few days, everything would seem to have been going well and I would begin to feel that maybe I was quite good at what is a ridiculously difficult job, but then, suddenly, I would fall off the side of the knife edge all doctors tread, by being too confident or too cautious, by not sending a child to hospital when I should have, or sending the child when it was not necessary, terrifying the family and wasting everyone's time. Then I would overcompensate and find myself falling off the other side of the knife edge before I finally managed to be back teetering along it again.

In his essay 'The Moment of Cubism' which is included in *The Sense of Sight*, John quoted from Apollinaire's last long poem 'La Jolie Russe':

> Pity us who fight continually on the frontiers
> Of the infinite and the future
> Pity for our mistakes pity for our sins.[3]

[2] Berger, J., and Mohr, J. *A Fortunate Man*. 1967. Penguin Books, 1969, p. 103.
[3] Berger, J. 'The Moment of Cubism'. In: *The Sense of Sight*. Vintage International, 1985, p. 170.

Apollinaire is reflecting his experience as a soldier who was severely wounded in the First World War. Weakened by the effects of war, he died of the so-called Spanish flu in November 1918, aged only thirty-eight. Reading this last poem, I think that many doctors working in a context of uncertainty and fear also feel that they are working on the frontiers of the infinite and the future, and know that they need to ask for pity for their mistakes.

In *About Looking*, John encouraged me to learn about doubt while looking at paintings, in this particular case, J. M. W. Turner's painting *The Burial at Sea*:

> The questions raised by the painting are moral—hence, as in many of Turner's later works, its somewhat claustrophobic quality—but the answers given are all ambivalent. No wonder that what Turner admired in painting was the ability to cast doubt, to throw into mystery. Rembrandt, he said admiringly, 'threw mysterious doubt over the meanest part of the common'.[4]

I like the ambition of throwing mysterious doubt over situations in which the general meets the particular as it does in every consultation. Many people are afraid of doubt and uncertainty but as Richard P. Feynman knew doubt brings freedom and room for manoeuvre: freedom to look and think again, to reconsider all possibilities over time and so minimize the chances of making a mistake. Later in that same speech, Feynman said:

> It is our responsibility as scientists, knowing the great progress which comes from a satisfactory philosophy of ignorance, the great progress which is the fruit of freedom of thought, to proclaim the value of this freedom; to teach how doubt is not to be feared but welcomed and discussed; and to demand this freedom as our duty to all coming generations.[5]

[4] Berger, J. *About Looking*. 1980. Bloomsbury Publishing, 2009, p152.
[5] Feynman, R. P. 'The Value of Science'. In: *What Do You Care What Other People Think?* 1988. Harper Collins, 1993, p. 248.

I think John would agree. In his essay 'A Story for Aesop' in *Keeping a Rendezvous*, he analyses the art of storytelling which suggests to me that it shares common ground with medicine. Looking at Velazquez's portrait of Aesop, painted around 1640, John wrote:

> Looking at him, I am reminded that I am not the first to pose unanswerable questions to myself, and I begin to share something of his composure: a curious composure for it coexists with hurt, with pain and with compassion. The last, essential for story-telling, is the complement of the original scepticism: a tenderness for experience, because it is human.[6]

Surely, this is the composure that I want as a doctor: a composure that can coexist with hurt and pain and compassion; a tenderness for and a profound interest in the life experience of my patients. I want to be able to see my patients with the same intensity and curiosity with which John saw paintings.

There is a passage in *And Our Faces* which took me completely by surprise when I first read it and which I have loved and thought about ever since, and which is also why I have already mentioned constellations at least twice:

> This is where stories began, under the aegis of that multitude of stars which at night filch certitudes and sometimes return them as faith. Those who first invented and then named the constellations were storytellers. Tracing an imaginary line between a cluster of stars gave them an image and an identity. The stars threaded on that line were like events threaded on a narrative. Imagining the constellations did not of course change the stars, nor did it change the

[6] Berger, J. 'A Story for Aesop. In: *Keeping a Rendezvous*. 1985. Vintage International, 1992, pp. 80–81.

black emptiness that surrounds them. What it changed was the way people read the night sky.[7]

I think that, among many other things this passage is about doubt. The storytellers who first named the constellations with stories that have lasted millennia could have threaded the stars differently and so created different images and different stories. What we see now is only one possible version of what there is to see. It is the same when a doctor considers the pattern of a patients' symptoms and wonders about an explanation. Is he or she seeing the familiar pattern of a familiar diagnosis or is the familiarity concealing a different possibility? I am back to valuing doubt as a safety device within every consultation. Could I be wrong? Was that diagnosis too easy? Am I missing something? And, most importantly, what does the patient him- or herself think? The feeling of doubt becomes a kind of sensor which can be cultivated to allow and encourage thinking and rethinking. Except in emergency situations, diagnoses should be made as slowly as possible through a reiterating process of reconsideration that extends over as much time as is reasonably available. It is dangerous whenever governments and policymakers put healthcare systems under such pressure that this becomes impossible.

[7] Berger, J. *And Our Faces, My Heart, Brief as Photos.* 1984. Vintage International, 1991, p. 8.

23

DEATH

John wrote a lot about death and we also talked and wrote to each other about it a lot. Most of what I learnt and thought as a result went into my book published in 2008 as *Matters of Life and Death* in English and, translated by Maria Nadotti, as *Modi di Morire* in Italian. I will try not to repeat myself here (and not entirely succeed) but neither John nor I stopped thinking about death after the books were published so there is a little more to say.

In July 2000, John gave the Peter Fuller Memorial Lecture at the Tate Modern in London. His subject was still life and his title was *The Infinity of Desire*. He discussed the work of Zurbarán, Chardin, Cézanne, Morandi, and Barceló. Miquel Barceló was the only living painter he mentioned and he said:

> His fruit, carcasses and fish offer no illusion of permanence. What he is painting with each thing that he handles is a moment, a phase, in a repeated cycle of seeding, flowering, fading, dying. The paintings make this clear. They do not celebrate what things look like. What they celebrate, accidents notwithstanding, is recurrence, and the secret of recurrence is mortality. Barceló's still lifes oppose the crass promises of consumerism with the insinuation of death and the respect which death demands.[1]

---

[1] Berger, J. 'The Infinity of Desire'. *The Guardian*, 13 July 2000. https://www.theguardian.com/culture/2000/jul/13/artsfeatures.art

In July 2001, near the beginning of our correspondence,[2] John encouraged me to think more about death:

> I would like very much to do something with you with death and with Spinoza? The eternal as distinct from the immortal. I dunno. But talking together we'd make a walk.

Although I started to read about Spinoza's thought, John and I never quite made this walk.

I replied:[3]

> I know nothing about Spinoza but I found an essay by TS Eliot in which he says that Spinoza shares with Blake, Homer, Æschylus, Dante, Villon (who?), Montaigne, and Shakespeare 'a peculiar honesty, which, in a world too frightened to be honest, is peculiarly terrifying'.

John persevered:[4]

> For S. there were 3 types of human knowledge, 3 ways of learning, 3 ways of living in and surviving the universe around us, which he believed to be a unified universe. 1. The knowledge of physical things—including our own bodies—which exist in space. These things are in constant interaction, they continually bang against each other. Each interaction is a kind of shock. We begin to learn about this as soon as we are born. Necessary knowledge but knowledge which is as ephemeral as the things themselves, which by their nature are continually changing. 2. The knowledge of how the reactions, caused by these shocks form systems, make predictions possible, etc. It is the knowledge of affects and effects. To use an image (which S. doesn't use) it is no longer the knowledge of the extensive earth (system 1) but of the sky. 3. The knowledge of the eternal, of that which includes infinity, of God who is every thing,

---

[2] 25 July 2001.
[3] 22 August 2001.
[4] 23 August 2001.

and which resides in us when we think of, contemplate, or struggle towards the essence of every thing which is not yet extended in space, and every thing which is so extended.

Within this last form of knowledge (which needs to be made clearer than I have made it) the eternal inhabits us. Alive, we are already in the eternal. (The premonition of how many poets before or after Spinoza!) In his system the eternal is a continuum, parallel to that of the mortal.

The task of philosophy is to help us to live in such a way that our minds are open to the maximum 'habitation of the eternal'. After death, that which was eternal in the dead person when alive, that which fed that person's essence with the essence of other things (only all essences are also the single essence of God), continues. What continues after death is that part of the eternal with which we lived when we were mortal.

Forgive me, Iona …

At this point, although John declared that his account was one of an 'ignorant hooligan', I have to admit to being baffled, feeling much more ignorant and more than a little daunted, but I tried to reply:[5]

Your laying out of Spinoza's three types of human knowledge is very helpful and I think that I begin to get somewhere … Clearly, dying is all about the third type of knowledge and suddenly I can see the problems that science has with this—and doctors—to the extent that they try to be scientists—because science works by interrogating and testing knowledge. This works for all of us with the first type of knowledge, and for many with the second type, but interrogation of the third type is answered only by silence. Which is what happens for the doctor caring for the dying person—in the end—there is no answer and no way of knowing what you did that was right and that helped and what you did or said that hurt or was crass. And if poetry is the stuff of the third sort of

[5] 29 August 2001.

knowledge which it must be, it brings us back to William Carlos Williams and the need to discover the poem of each life and the poetry we share—which is perhaps the cause to die for—because it is only poetry that 'will look at what we both have to look at when both of us are no longer anywhere'.[6] And if that is the case, then it is the dying, as well as the poets, who must undertake Eliot's 'extraordinary labour of simplification',[7] which seems right. Is there any sense here or have I missed it altogether?

Several weeks later, in the aftermath of the 9/11 attacks on the United States and amid all the ill-considered and ill-fated talk about the 'forces of evil', I wrote[8] again:

Continuing on the trail of Spinoza started by you, I found this by George Santayana:

Somehow it gives man a sense of dignity and self-satisfaction to believe that his interests are those of the universe, and his likes and dislikes those of God; but this faith Spinoza would have us abandon. A doctrine which bids us lay down our lives and gives us, meantime, the assurance that our cause is absolutely just and our adversary's cause absolutely unjust, demands a smaller sacrifice than a doctrine which bids us keep our lives and give up that assurance.

—which needs, so urgently, to be heard by both sides of the current divide.

More than twenty years has elapsed since we wrote these letters and I think that only now, I begin to understand John's distinction between the immortal and the eternal.

---

[6] From: Juarroz, R. Poesie vertical (I–IV). Talus d'approche, 1996. Translated from the French by John Berger.
[7] Eliot, T. S. The Sacred Wood: Essays on Poetry and Criticism. 1920. Methuen & Co Ltd, p. 137.
[8] 20 October 2001.

For Spinoza, there is no personal immortality beyond death. All the individual benefits of human knowledge and effort can only be realized within each lifetime because there is nothing beyond death, neither rewards in heaven nor punishments in hell. There is no immortality; yet eternity is to be found in human thought and ideas because all thought has the potential to contribute to the totality of ideas, so rendering them eternal.[9] People die but ideas are kept alive by repetition or development and so become eternal. In a strange and beautiful way, writing this, I feel part of this mysterious process. In seventeenth-century Amsterdam, Spinoza drew a distinction between the immortal and the eternal. His ideas have been perpetuated by many subsequent writers, including, John and now I am playing my small part in this wonder by seeking to keep John's ideas alive. And so, perhaps in some sense, we have finally made the walk that John proposed.

Back in 2001, John was worried[10] about a very good friend who was dying of cancer in London:

> The new sessions of chemotherapy. It must be such a difficult auditing job. To measure the pain caused, the violence submitted to, in exchange for how many additional weeks of active life. And I think what you think is that, in his case, and given his need to resist, it is worth it. Am I right? Or the more peaceful alternative?

I replied:[11]

> I agree about the difficulty of weighing up the usefulness of more chemotherapy and I suspect that you and I might make a different decision—although who really knows until they are right up

[9] Nadler, S. *Spinoza's Heresy: Immortality and the Jewish Mind*. Oxford University Press, 2001.
[10] 4 August 2001.
[11] 29 August 2001.

against it?—but I think for —, it really is a part of his strategy of resistance.

After his friend had died, John wrote:[12]

Forgive my silence. I have been so discouraged. (I don't like the word depressed. It has no fight in it.) Me, I'm fighting, but, for the moment, beaten. People skidding out of their mind. People drinking themselves to anger. Age lowering my resistance. Cowardice encouraging cowardice—my own included.

The following month I replied:[13]

I am not only sorry and sad that you are so discouraged but worried too … You seem to be talking about a lot of losses and it seems to me that people become ill and die at the point when they have sustained a critical number of losses—sometimes losses of health, sometimes losses of more nebulous things like honour (remember the red on the Finnish angel) or reputation—but most often losses of love. And people are more or less resilient and have greater or lesser reserves of love and health and honour, and for some who start with very little, only a little loss can be already critical. And—it is obvious that the older one gets the more losses one must suffer—particularly of those who are loved and loving.

Later, in the same letter, I wrote:

So all this is a long and ramblingly ineffective way of saying that I hope more than I can say that you are finding reserves of love and the courage to believe once again in 'the fair adventure of tomorrow'. (We saw [Shakespeare's] King John the evening before last).

In 2002, David and I spent a few days in Paris and, before going I asked John a variant of my ten books question: if you could

12 26 December 2001.
13 7 January 2002.

only see three paintings in Paris, which three would they be? The answer came by fax:[14]

> Pictures to look at? I immediately think of very obvious ones. Caravaggio's <u>Death of the Virgin</u> in the Louvre [it's about the role of red perhaps not in death but in our ideas of death.] Courbet's <u>The Burial at Ornans</u> by Courbet in the Orsay Museum [About bereavement and earth, soil. The most anti-cremation statement I know.] A few Fayum portraits—in the Egyptian section of the Louvre. Also in the Egyptian section the mummy-cases (painted)—you can almost get inside one. AND—what you really shouldn't miss—an extraordinary Egyptian walking couple, carved out of acacia (one piece). It is one of the most <u>alive</u> sculptures I have ever seen, and they are walking towards (amongst other things) death, and they know it. An image where the tenderness of desire and mortality are inseparable. And, finally, in the Flemish section of the paintings in the Louvre—a descent from the Cross by Dirk Bouts. The landscape behind the Cross is like (if I remember correctly) a death at noon.

On our return, I wrote:[15]

> We had a very good day on Sunday and found all of your pictures. It feels important to try and write about them and to find my way. Deleuze, in his book on Spinoza [which John had encouraged me to read], quotes a passage from Malamud's *The Fixer*, which talks about Spinoza's attempt to find freedom by thinking things through and connecting everything up.
>
> For me, the three paintings are all about those who are left behind, which seems right, because this is the only experience of death that we can recount—the experience of having been abandoned by the dead. You mentioned the dog in the Courbet. Why is he looking away? Somehow his turned head links to all the obscured human faces—not only the weeping women but also the bowed heads of the pall bearers. Or is he looking to someone

[14] 14 March 2002.
[15] 11 April 2002.

in particular for reassurance that cannot be given—as one of the children does? I'm not sure.

The Dirk Bouts painting is full of pain. For me, it is the only one that conveys the suffering of dying—or, in this case, of being killed. Christ's mouth is still so tense and so obviously parched. And his mother's face manages to combine the agony of loss with a palpable sense of relief that the suffering is over—that the pain makes death welcome.

...

And then the Caravaggio—again there is so much sadness in the faces of the living and only peace for the dead. But why is the red so shocking? The red dress seems to have sucked all the red out of her body making it lifeless. And the blackness of the blanket?

We walked past Géricault's *The Raft of the Medusa* which has the horrifying image of the man who is still alive but who, because of the loss of the young man whose body he holds, (is it his son?), has lost all interest in being rescued, in continuing to live. It has all the awful life-sapping desolation of loss.

And we looked at the Fayum portraits again and rediscovered their astonishing directness and immediacy. It becomes a tangible confrontation between individual human beings across millennia—somehow intensely Spinozan. But why do the portraits convey that immediacy whereas the sculptured heads just don't? It is something to do with the eyes—but what?

And we looked again at the Goya portrait of the Marquise de Solana and, for the first time, I noticed that it was painted very shortly before she died and that it is extraordinarily like the Fayum portraits with the same steady directness in the gaze which is almost naked in its vulnerability but at the same time, inexplicably, conveys enormous strength.

And, finally the walking couple carved of a single piece of acacia [carved sometime between 2350 and 2200 BCE] which, because we would not have found it without your direction, felt like a gift from you. So much tenderness in the touch of the woman on the man's back and arm and the courageous commitment to life, death and each other in the unflinching gaze. And the transience and fragility of everything emphasised by the eating away of the wood.

Thank you.

Just a week later, John replied:[16]

Sciatica gone—walked out to buy a paper and never came back.

How right you are about the Marquise de Solana. She really does have the expression of a Fayum portrait. She died at 28. She was, I guess, 27, when Goya painted her. She knew she was fatally ill? (But look at her feet. What flamenco insolence!) Your insight makes me wonder about something else. Maybe quite a few of Goya's portraits have this Fayum resemblance. Given the history of the Peninsular War in Spain—the first 'modern war' in certain respects—many were living with a heightened sense of mortality. Only in Goya is there this Fayum correspondence.

John sent me a copy of *Keeping a Rendezvous* which was out of print at the time. I wrote[17] to John:

In 'Christ of the Peasants' [an essay about the pilgrim photographs of Markéta Luskačová], you write about how we have become ashamed of our consanguinity with the Dead. And then in *A Fortunate Man*, you write:

The doctor is the familiar of death. When we call for a doctor, we are asking him to cure us and to relieve our suffering, but, if he cannot cure us, we are also asking him to witness our dying. The value of the witness is that he has seen so many others die… . He is the living intermediary between us and the multitudinous dead. He belongs to us and he has

---

[16] 17 April 2002.
[17] 16 July 2002.

belonged to them. And the hard but real comfort which they offer through him is still that of fraternity.[18]

And thinking about these two things together, I realise how, for me, Kentish Town is populated by generations of ghosts—waiting in half-remembered interiors—alongside the changed rooms and the new inhabitants. The total population of living and dead gets denser and denser. It must be the same for you in the village. Have we really forgotten—isn't it the same for everyone to a greater or lesser extent? Isn't it just that we have forgotten how to talk about it?

Much later, John wrote[19] to me describing his struggle in the face of his wife Beverly's terminal illness:

There is the shock of an announced illness.

There is the shock of institutionalised medicine with its recorded speeches and no voice.

Both of these one can, to some extent, argue oneself around, and negotiate.

And then there is the inner imaginative shock before which one is supine. And so the shock multiplies, reproducing itself in mode after mode. An inner mob touched by a contagious fear. And your energy is smothered or, more accurately, seeks oblivion. Wakefulness is too menacing. You shuffle into a fabricated senility.

Of course I cope. Cook, drive, shop, accompany Beverly, talk, listen, but the fatality inside me is a spell cast upon me—and I can't find the counter-measures. And instead of rising to the occasion, I diminish. I can do nothing, see nothing, properly. I've never experienced such a state before. Because my resources have vanished. I have only a shift covering me.

You told me to write, so I write this to you. It's self-indulgent. I suppose it will pass. A voicelessness.

[18] Berger, J., and Mohr, J. *A Fortunate Man.* 1967. Penguin Books, 1969, p. 68.
[19] 18 February 2012.

Most doctors have encountered people in this particular state of shock and anguish but very few have heard such an acute and intimate description. It is not by any measure self-indulgent and, quite on the contrary, it is courageous and it has the capacity to help others, patients, doctors and the imminently bereaved, to feel less alone. He was never voiceless.

Faced with his despair, I was reminded of what he himself wrote in G.:

> Write anything. Truth or untruth, it is unimportant. Speak but speak with tenderness, for that is all that you can do that may help a little. Build a barricade of words, no matter what they mean. Speak so that he can be aware of your presence. Speak so that he knows that you are there not feeling his pain. Say anything, for his pain is larger than any distinction you can make between truth and untruth. Dress him with the words of your voice as others dress his wounds. Yes. Here and now. It will stop.[20]

This is in turn reminds me of my mother-in-law who lost her husband and the love of her life when she was only forty-eight and he only fifty-six. After he died, she divided her friends into two groups, those who acknowledged her loss, more or less adequately, and those who said nothing or seemed to pretend that nothing had really happened. She taught me that it is always better to say or write something, anything, rather than nothing.

---

[20] Berger, J. G. 1972. Bloomsbury Publishing, 1996, p. 75.

24

ANGELS

John liked the notion of angels and thought about them in relation to everything either evanescent or eternal, mysterious and numinous, and particularly, in relation to the tenderness of both affection and love. They appear often in his letters and in his drawings.

In a letter to me,[1] he used the word in relation to Maria Nadotti who translated all his writing into Italian:

> Maria N. is truly mysterious, which is why I call her Angel. Mysterious because without any of the usual string-pulling she persuades things to happen—large complicated things that usually require removal men!

In the *Shape of the Pocket*, John found angels invoked by compassion:

> Compassion has no place in the natural order of the world, which operates on the basis of necessity. The laws of necessity are as unexceptional as the laws of gravitation. The human faculty of compassion opposes this order and is therefore best thought of as being in some way supernatural. To forget oneself, however briefly, to identify with a stranger to the point of fully recognising her or him, is to defy necessity, and in this defiance, even if small and quiet ... there

---

[1] 20 March 2008.

is a power which cannot be measured by the limits of the natural order. It is not a means and it has no end.[2]

In the summer of 2001, David and I took a road trip around the forests and lakes of Finland with the aim of seeing as many buildings as possible designed by Alvar Aalto. A small diversion took us to see Petäjävesi old church which has been on the UNESCO World Heritage List since 1994. Inside there is an astonishingly beautiful wooden pulpit decorated with crudely carved wooden angels and I sent John a postcard of the lone angel who hovers above the preacher on the sounding board of the pulpit.

John responded,[3] writing down the side of a letter: 'I love, love, love your Finnish angel.'

A little later, John sent me this photo of the postcard with questions written on the back:

Questions for Iona. With love John.

The Finnish angel. Isn't her first admission (and she has just been admitted, no?) about her relative powerlessness? What is startling (reassuringly startling) is that this in no way diminishes her caring and her concern.

The red is perhaps rose, her cheeks pink rose, but it might be blood? Why is blood so closely associated with honour?

I see that this is another example of John's characteristic juxtaposition of two apparently contradictory words: reassuringly startling. The combination is surprising and sets up a tension which makes me try to work out more precisely what he

---

[2] Berger, J. 'A Man with Tousled Hair'. In: Berger, J. *The Shape of the Pocket*. Bloomsbury, 2001, p. 179.
[3] 25 July 2001.

means. I ask myself whether 'startlingly reassuring' would mean something different from 'reassuringly startling' And I'm still not sure.

I replied:[4]

> I too can see the anxiety and diffidence of the new recruit in our Finnish angel—but, although she is new, she is determined not to flinch and to look at things straight on and not to turn away. Which brings back your perception of the doctor and the patient not looking at each other in the eyes—and since we talked about this and the more I look at the angel, I am aware of when I avoid looking, when I flinch.
>
> ...
>
> The angel made me think of flinching and this is not a word that I use very often and so I wondered about it and looked in the OED and made a serendipitous discovery of this quotation:
>
>> 1817 W. Taylor in *Monthly Rev.* **83** 498 That unwelcome flinch which the touch of egotism gives to benevolence.
>
> Somehow, it couldn't be more apt.

Some time in spring 2002, I sent John a picture of another, slightly more sophisticated angel—this time a Swedish one, which we found standing in the wooden church in the small town of Ekshärad.

John acknowledged[5] this new angel:

> Thank you for the Swedish angel, who has the colouring, no?, of a dove. Why do you say she's threatening us with time? Perhaps she is—and I haven't seen her in her setting—but it seems to me that she might just as well be carrying the burden of time for us! Promising that which is beyond time.

---

[4] 5 August 2001.
[5] 8 May 2002.

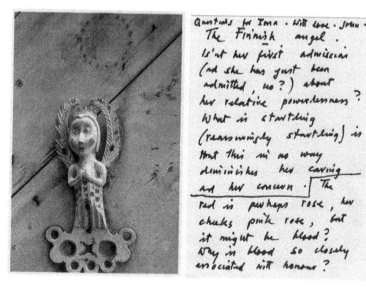

Figure 9 Postcard with message from John Berger
Source: © John Berger and John Berger Estate.

And I am struck by the typical generosity of John's assessment compared to mine.

In 2006, he wrote an essay about Pier Paolo Pasolini's 1963 film *La Rabbia*.[6] It begins:

> If I say he was like an angel, I can't imagine anything more stupid being said about him. An angel painted by Cosimo Tura? No. There's a St. George by Tura which is his speaking likeness! He abhorred official saints and beatific angels. So why say it? Because his habitual and immense sadness allowed him to share jokes, and the look on his distressed face distributed laughter, guessing exactly who needed it most. And the more intimate his touch, the more lucid it became! He could whisper to people softly about the worst that was happening to them and they somehow suffered less. '. . . for we never have despair without some small hope'.

[6] Berger, J. 'The Chorus in Our Heads or Pier Paolo Pasolini'. *Vertigo*. 2006, 3(3): 77–83.

'Disperazone senza unpo' di speranza.'—Pier Paolo Pasolini
(1922–1975).

I think he doubted many things about himself, but never his gift of
prophesy which was, perhaps, the one thing he would have liked to
have doubted. Yet, since he was prophetic, he comes to our aid in
what we are living today. I have just watched a film made in 1963.
Astonishingly it was never publicly shown. It arrives like a prover-
bial message put in a bottle and washed up forty years later on our
beach.

Later he concludes:

> La Rabbia is a film of love. Yet its lucidity is comparable to that in
> Kafka's aphorism: 'The Good is, in a certain sense, comfortless.'
> This is why I say Pasolini was like an angel.

I wrote[7] to thank John for sending me a Christmas present of
his book, with the photographer Marc Trivier, about Giacometti,
titled My Beautiful:

> Thank you for sending me your wonderful new book which I
> have read and read again. The photos are hauntingly beautiful and
> indeed the whole book seems to be about feeling haunted and that
> this is a good—a life enhancing—thing. I wonder why haunting
> has come to have negative connotations.
>
> And once again you have changed the world for me. It makes me
> think again of Seamus Heaney writing:
>
>> The world is different after it has been read by a Shakespeare
>> or an Emily Dickinson or a Samuel Beckett because it has
>> been augmented by their reading of it.[8]
>
> And it seems that every time you pick up your pen to write
> about an artist—Modigliani, Goya, Masaccio, Géricault—and now

---

[7] 12 January 2005.
[8] Heaney, S. The Redress of Poetry. Faber & Faber, 1995, p. 159.

Giacometti, you make the world different and you make my seeing of it richer.... The place where you write:

> The irreducible was Giacometti's ideal. His figures are there, with what is left after air and light and usage have dispersed with the rest. They are like skeletons? The opposite. They concern what anatomy can never categorise or identify. They show how in the depths of the body, there is an interface, a shared skin between the physical and metaphysical.[9]

is magical for me—my work, when I do it well, is at that interface.

In his essay 'The White Bird' in *The Sense of Sight*, John compared art to prayer:

> The evolution of natural forms and the evolution of human perception have coincided to produce the phenomenon of a potential recognition: what is and what we can see (and by seeing also feel) sometimes meet at a point of affirmation.
>
> ...
>
> All the languages of art have been developed as an attempt to transform the instantaneous into the permanent. Art supposes that beauty is not an exception—is not in despite of—but is the basis for an order.
>
> ...
>
> Art does not imitate nature, it imitates a creation, sometimes to propose an alternative world, sometimes simply to amplify, to confirm, to make social the brief hope offered by nature. Art is an organized response to what nature allows us to glimpse occasionally. Art sets out to transform the potential recognition into an unceasing one. It proclaims man in the hope of receiving a surer reply ... the transcendental face of art is always a form of prayer.[10]

[9] Berger, J., and Trivier, M. My Beautiful. Centre Régional de la Photographie, Nord Pas-de-Calais, 2004, p. 31.
[10] Berger, J. 'The White Bird'. In: *The Sense of Sight*. 1985. Vintage International, 1993, pp. 8–9.

Figure 10 Photograph by Iona Heath of the interior of Ekshärad church, Sweden
Source: Author.

In *A Fortunate Man*, describing general practitioners like his Dr Sassall, and, I hope, as I tried to be, John wrote:

> They are driven by the need to know. The patient is their material. Yet to them, more than to any other doctor, the patient, in his totality is for that very reason sacred.[11]

I think John was a man who sensed angels everywhere. Responding to my report of our visit to Paris: he wrote:[12]

> The red in the Caravaggio. The red is the colour (in his life), which sees that between desire and death there is no frontier at all. Therefore it is the transcendental colour. (For the Renaissance blue was this colour.) Here (perhaps? tell me?) Caravaggio outwits—with a cardsharper's trick—Gadamer's otherwise so wise argument.
>
> All the time I'm avoiding your true concern: how to give attention, the one they need, to the dying? Perhaps sometimes a third person comes in. Not only body and mind. (And this I suspect is already in Spinoza and his discoveries) but an angel—a desire whose light has changed colour?

A week later, I replied:[13]

> And—yes—desire offers us protection from tragedy and pain—it offers us our glimpse of heaven and, if I understand Deleuze on Spinoza, this glimpse is what heaven is. Occurring always in the present—never in the future. But doesn't desire always contain within it the fear of its ending? How is one ever to survive the loss of one's partner in desire? It is perhaps possible if the desire is lost before the person—but otherwise this must be the worst thing that we ever have to face—the loss of our glimpse of heaven.
>
> And so—yes—with Caravaggio—in a shared transcendence, there is no frontier between desire and death—but because one

[11] Berger, J., and Mohr, J. *A Fortunate Man.* 1967. Penguin Books, 1969, p. 80.
[12] 17 April 2002.
[13] 24 April 2002.

occurs in time and the other is timeless, the barrier is also absolute. Desire breaches the barrier—allows us a sense of both timelessness and heaven—but, in the end, it is confined by time. The red in the Caravaggio seems to show both sides of this contradiction.

I finally realised that I could not continue to resist the direction that you have been gently pushing me in for months—and that I must acknowledge that I cannot continue to think about death and dying without making some accommodation with a notion of God. My resistance is partly to do with an unpleasantly evangelistic religious phase in my adolescence (I used to sing rousing hymns around the house in the hope of converting my brothers—I must have been unbearable) and in contrast to this I have found the starkness of a kind of atheism comforting. And religion has been and continues to be such a force for evil in the world. But I think that I begin to understand the Spinozan view of an immanent god within nature and within the human imagination. I treasure this quotation from the Deleuze book on Spinoza that you suggested:

> the eternity of essence does not come afterwards; it is strictly contemporaneous, coexistent with existence in duration.... the good or strong individual is the one who exists so fully or so intensely that he has gained eternity in his lifetime, so that death, always extensive, always external, is of little significance to him. The ethical test is therefore the contrary of the deferred judgement.[14]

which somehow evokes what Seamus Heaney said at the Memorial Service for Ted Hughes:

> One part of Ted believed in the gene and its laws as the reality we inhabit and are bound to adjust to, since there issues from the genetic code the whole alphabet of our possibilities, from the alpha at the start of the evolutionary journey to omega at the end. But another part of him looked through the microscope and telescope into the visionary crystal, and could see Dante's eternal margherita, the pearl of foreverness, in the

[14] Deleuze, G. *Spinoza: Practical Philosophy*. 1970. San Francisco: City Lights Books, 1988, pp. 40–41.

interstices of the DNA. This is the part of him that recognised that myths and fairy tales were the poetic code, that the body was a spirit beacon as well as a chemical formula, that it was born for both ecstasy and extinction.[15]

[15] https://www.theguardian.com/theobserver/1999/may/16/featuresreview.review2

FAREWELL

Towards the end of October 2016, I posted my last letter[1] to John, less than three months before he died:

I've been writing to you in my head about so many things and for so many months that it is hard to know where to begin. Last Monday, we went to the poetry event celebrating your coming birthday with poems by the amazing Bejan Matur and Lavinia Greenlaw. Toby Jones read your poems beautifully—you would have enjoyed them! Bejan described your writing about imprisonment and torture as being exactly true to her own terrible experience—and it reminded me of how your writing about being a general practitioner is exactly true to my own so much more fortunate experience. I think this is your genius: your ability to imagine and capture in words other people's experience—so that they themselves can recognise it. It is a wonderful gift.

Sadly, Amarjit Chandan was not able to be there. Do you remember that you showed me a book of his poems when I was with you in Antony? I copied out these two lines:

The paper is the window to the present moment in time.
It is the gateway to the possibility.

In his Afterword to *A Fortunate Man*, added after John Sassall's suicide in 1981, John wrote:

A man's life is utterly transformed by his death.
Death changes the facts qualitatively but not quantitatively. One does not know more facts about a man because he is dead. But what one already knows hardens and becomes definite. We cannot hope for ambiguities to be clarified, we cannot hope for further change, we

---

[1] 23 October 2016.

cannot hope for more. We are now the protagonists and we have to make up our minds.

This is irreversibly true and yet I have continued to write to him in my head and I suspect the many others who were fortunate enough to be counted a friend have done the same. Yet the actual correspondence has come to its inevitable end and I miss its joys and its challenges.

As the reader will have noted, I take a lot of inspiration from quotations and I fear that I could easily be counted among 'the "quote and dote" school of sherry-sipping sensitive souls', so acutely described in a review by Declan Kiberd, professor of Irish Studies at University of Notre Dame, published in the *Dublin Review of Books* in February 2021.[2] Yet within our correspondence John was generous enough not to let this happen by never taking anything at face value and almost always responding at a different level and, so often, making me think again.

In his preface to *John Berger: A Season in London, 2005*, Geoff Dyer wrote:

Irrespective of disparities of age or talent John longs for ... No, let me rephrase that, he simply has no patience for any relationships that are not relationships of equality. More than any of its perks or privileges John has enjoyed his success because it has allowed this predisposition to be absolutely confirmed. There is nothing humble about this: it's just that the potential of a hierarchical relationship with the world is exhausted in the instant that it is established.[3]

This describes my experience precisely. Quite remarkably, like many other of his collaborators and correspondents, I never felt condescended to or in any way intimidated. This gift for relationships of equality is invaluable and sets a high bar for those of us who hope to emulate it. Part of it, was his generous sharing of his friends, to which I now owe my enduring friendships with Maria Nadotti and John Christie, artist, cameraman, and director, who corresponded with John to create the two wonderful books *I Send You This Cadmium Red* and *Lapwing and Fox*.

I tried to thank John Berger on several occasions including when I told him that I had been reading Italo Calvino's *Invisible Cities*. I wrote:[4]

---

[2] https://drb.ie/articles/quote-dont-dote/
[3] Dyer, G. 'Preface'. In: *John Berger: A Season in London*, 2005, Artevents, p. 10.
[4] 7 November 2002.

The end of the Italo Calvino is:

> The inferno of the living is not something that will be: if there is one, it is what is already here, the inferno that we live every day, that we form by being together. There are two ways to escape suffering it. The first is easy for many: accept the inferno and become such a part of it that you no longer see it. The second is risky and demands constant vigilance and apprehension: seek and learn to recognize who and what, in the midst of the inferno, are not inferno, then make them endure, give them space.[5]

Somehow this second course seems to describe your life's work.

Several years later, I described[6] a ridiculous dream:

> I have been dreaming rather vividly recently—I have no idea why—and a few nights ago I dreamt that you gave me an enormous boat-shaped and almost boat-sized apricot tart! That would appear to say something about greed and love of apricot tart but also seems to give some measure of everything you have given me over the years—ideas and words and courage and drawings and friends and love—all measured out in apricot tart.

Thank you, John.

---

[5] Calvino, I. Invisible Cities. 1972. Vintage, 1997, p. 165.
[6] 31 August 2008.

PERMISSIONS

With thanks to the John Berger Estate for permission to quote from the following texts:

Text for *Markéta Luskačová: Pilgrims*. Arts Council of Great Britain, © John Berger and John Berger Estate, 1985.

'The Infinity of Desire'. *The Guardian*, 13 July 2000. https://www.theguardian.com/culture/2000/jul/13/ artsfeatures.art, © John Berger and John Berger Estate, 2000.

'Dispatches: Undefeated Despair'. *Race & Class*, © John Berger and John Berger Estate, 2006.

Berger, J., and Grant, S., 'Walking Back Home' in Killip, C. *In Flagrante*. © John Berger and John Berger Estate, 1988.

'Caravaggio: A Contemporary View' in *Studio International* 1983, volume 196, number 998. © John Berger and John Berger Estate, 1983.

Berger, J., and Trivier, M., *My Beautiful*. Centre Regional de la Photographie, Nord Pas-de-Calais, © John Berger and John Berger Estate, 2004, p. 31.

Art and Revolution, © John Berger and John Berger Estate, 1969 (UK and Commonwealth).

A Seventh Man, © John Berger and John Berger Estate, 1975.

Keeping a Rendezvous, © John Berger and John Berger Estate, 1992 (UK and Commonwealth).

The Sense of Sight, © John Berger and John Berger Estate, 1985 (UK and Commonwealth).

John Berger's personal letters to Iona Heath.

Thanks also to the following publishers for permission to quote from the following publications:

A Fortunate Man by John Berger, 1967, reproduced by kind permission of Canongate (UK and Commonwealth).

ACKNOWLEDGEMENTS

First of all, to John Berger for his wisdom, his encouragement, his generous friendship, and his fearless political stance on behalf of the exploited and the disinherited.

Then to Yves, Katya, Jacob, and the Estate for so generously allowing me to quote freely from John's writings and from his personal letters to me, and, again, for allowing me to include some of the drawings that he sent to me over the years.

To Teresa Pintó, John's literary agent, for all the work she did to grant me the necessary permissions. And to Nora Bériou, the John Berger Estate secretary, for all her help and support.

To John Christie for having been a wonderful friend and support for many years.

To Maria Nadotti for translating John's work into Italian and tirelessly promoting it, for believing in me unswervingly since we first met, for offering me the same unbelievable service, albeit on a minuscule scale, and for allowing me to include her photo of John in Palestine in 2005. This book is dedicated to her.

To Philip Davis who first invited me to write this book and who, since then, has been so fulsome in his support, encouragement, and gentle editing suggestions.

To Bill Johncocks for his brilliant work on the index and for drawing attention to several inconsistencies, his delightful word for what were clearly mistakes.

To Gavin Francis and Esa Aldegheri for their generous hospitality and support.

To Gareth Evans for his tireless enthusiasm and for everything he does.

To the British Journal of General Practice for permission to quote the whole of Marshall Marinker's report of John Berger's John Hunt Lecture in January 2000.

And to David for his love, and for putting up with me, believing in me, and helping me with the illustrations.

INDEX

For the benefit of digital users, indexed terms that span two pages (e.g., 52–53) may, on occasion, appear on only one of those pages.

Note: Separately published writings by John Berger are collected following his name, unless they are treated extensively enough to require subentry analysis. JB's essays and periodical articles appear at their titles.